QUEEN ELIZABETH II

A Glorious 70 Years

Alison James

sona
BOOKS

First Published Danann Media Publishing 2022

WARNING: For private domestic use only, any unauthorised Copying, hiring, lending or public performance of this book is illegal.

CAT NO: SON0522

Photography courtesy of

Getty images:

Joe Giddens / Pool / AFP
Culture Club
Hulton Deutsch
Lisa Sheridan / Hulton Archive
Keystone
Anwar Hussein / WireImage
George Rinhart / Corbis
The Print Collector
Sahm Doherty Universal History
Archive / Universal Images
Fox Photos
British Combine

Topical Press Agency
Popperfoto
Chris Jackson
Mark Cuthbert / UK Press
Julian Parker
Tim Graham
Ullstein Bild
Central Press / Stringer
Topical Press Agency
Tony Evans / Timelapse Library Ltd
Vatican Pool
Digital Studio / TV Times

R. Brigden / Stringer
Mathieu Polak
WPA Pool / Pool
John Giles
Daniel Leal / AFP
Steve Parsons
Max Mumby / Indigo
Bettmann
Anna Clopet / Corbis
Ian Gavan

All other images, Wiki Commons

Book cover design Darren Grice at Ctrl-d

Layout design Alex Young at Cre81ve

Juliette O'Neill and Tom O'Neill Copy Editors

Made in EU.

ISBN: 978-1-912918-87-4

Contents

Introduction

The lyrics of the first verse of the United Kingdom and Commonwealth National Anthem

The national anthem of Great Britain was adopted as such in September 1745, during the reign of King George II who ruled for 33 years. Now, 237 years later, we are celebrating the 70-year reign of his great, great, great, great, great, great, great granddaughter – Her Majesty Queen Elizabeth the Second, by the Grace of God, of the United Kingdom of Great Britain and Northern Ireland and of Her other Realms and Territories Queen, Head of the Commonwealth, Defender of the Faith. She is the first British monarch in history to reach the truly formidable milestone of a Platinum Jubilee so what better time to look back with gratitude and love at the 70 years of her reign – a time of unparalleled change and unexpected challenges. Her Majesty's commitment to duty and service has never faltered as she's ruled – and continues to rule - with dignity, good grace, kindness and wisdom. Thank you, ma'am.

God save our gracious Queen,
Long live our noble Queen,
God save the Queen!
Send her victorious,
Happy and glorious,
Long to reign over us,
God save the Queen!

Above:

Queen Elizabeth II cuts a cake to celebrate
the start of the Platinum Jubilee during a
reception in the Ballroom of Sandringham
House, the Queen's Norfolk residence on
February 5, 2022

Above:
Proud parents Queen Elizabeth II
and Prince Phillip riding in an open
carriage en-route to Westminster
Abbey for the wedding of their
son Prince Andrew to Miss Sarah
Ferguson

The Princess Elizabeth

Winston Churchill

'She has an air of authority and reflectiveness that is astonishing'

Born April 21 1926, Queen Elizabeth II is the first British monarch to ever have been born in a private house rather than Royal Castle, Palace or Mansion. With building works ongoing at the London mansion rented by her parents, the Duke and Duchess of York, the mother-to-be preferred to give birth at the Mayfair home of her parents rather than her in-laws' Palace. It was not an easy birth. The baby was breech and the Duchess in labour for the best part of a day. A girl was finally born by Caesarian Section at 2.40am. She was third in line to the throne after her father and her Uncle David, the future King Edward VIII, but there was never any supposition that she would one day ascend the throne.

Baby York was the apple of her parents' eye.

'You don't know what a tremendous joy it is to Elizabeth and me to have our little girl,' the Duke wrote to his mother, Queen Mary, on the day of his daughter's birth. *'We always wanted a child to make our happiness complete and now that it has at last happened, it seems so wonderful and strange.'*

Queen Mary was equally smitten, far more so than she had ever been with her own children. *'The baby is a little darling,'* she wrote, *'with a lovely complexion and pretty fair hair.'*

Above:
Portrait of Elizabeth II as a baby held by her mother, Elizabeth (1900-2002). After the painting by John Helier Lander

Right:
The young Princess Elizabeth, 1928

Below:

The Duke and Duchess of York with their baby daughter after her christening in the private chapel at Buckingham Palace, where she received the names Elizabeth Alexandra Mary

Right:

The Duchess of York with her newborn daughter Princess

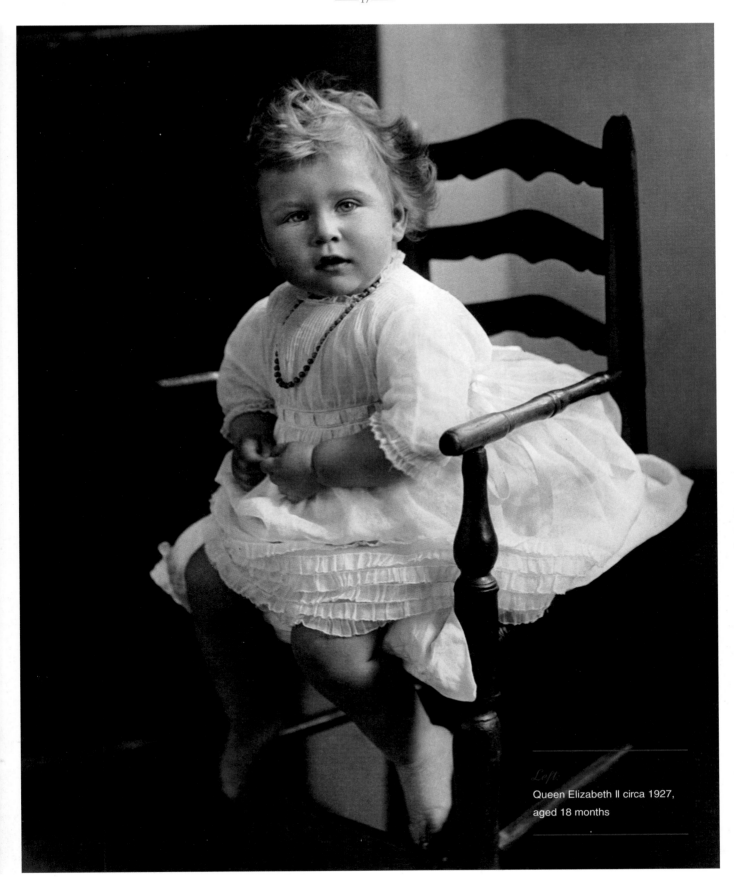

Left:
Queen Elizabeth II circa 1927,
aged 18 months

'The little darling' was christened Elizabeth after her mother, Alexandra after her great grandmother Queen Alexandra who had died the previous year, and Mary after her grandmother. Baby Elizabeth apparently cried so much at her christening that 'her nurse dosed her with dill water' - a remedy containing alcohol back in the 1920s – much to the amusement of her Uncle David.

Nanny immediately took charge with the Duchess of York's own childhood nurse, Clara Knight, caring for baby Elizabeth. Known as 'Alah', Clara raised her charge in the same time-honoured way she had brought up the baby's mother. She and Elizabeth lived in a suite of 'sunny' rooms at the top of Yorks' house in Mayfair, London, consisting of

Above:

Princess Elizabeth on the Time Magazine cover, April 29, 1929

Right:

Princess Elizabeth at age seven, portrait by Philip de László, 1933

---

a day nursery, a night nursery and a bathroom linked by a landing, with wide windows looking down on the park. It was a loving and calm yet neat and ordered environment, and discipline was the order of the day. A strict routine was adhered to at all times with periods set aside for feeding, bathing, playing, perambulator walks and parental visits.

Queen Mary and King George were doting grandparents to the 'Bambino', as the Queen called her. Mary would often send a car to fetch baby Elizabeth at teatime and 'Bambino' would be shown off the Queen's guests with the doting Grandmama describing the child as a 'white fluff of thistledown' who had 'the sweetest air of complete serenity'.

When Elizabeth was nine-months-old, her parents were sent on an official tour of Australia and New Zealand – a trip undertaken by sea that would take them away from their baby daughter for six months. But rather than being chastised by the public for leaving her not-yet-one-year-old, the Duchess was applauded for doing her Royal and wifely duty. She was however upset at the prospect of leaving little Elizabeth for so long. 'Feeling very miserable at leaving the baby,' she wrote on the morning of departure. 'Went up and played with her and she was so sweet, playing with the buttons on Bertie's jacket quite broke me up. Luckily she doesn't realize anything.'

Baby Elizabeth was left in the care of Alah and her paternal grandparents. Queen Mary saw her grand-daughter at least three times a day and it was she who held the baby when she made her first balcony appearance when she was just a year-old. Meanwhile King George V, who had never allowed his own children to speak to him unless he addressed them first, was happy to have 'Lilibet', as she lispily called herself, clamber onto his lap and pull his beard. She was without doubt his favourite grandchild and he always requested that she be seated next to him at meal times.

Princess Elizabeth was on her way to becoming a mini superstar. Aged just two-and-a-half, Winston Churchill declared on meeting her for the first time that, 'She is a character. She has an air of authority and reflectiveness that is astonishing in an infant'. By the time she was three, she was on the cover of 'Time' magazine, dressed in her trademark yellow rather than the traditional pink

for a girl. This set a trend for little girls – and boys – the world over. There was tangible disappointment when the Duchess of York arrived on an official visit to Edinburgh without her daughter. *'I fear it has been a very great disappointment to our people,'* she wrote to Queen Mary. *'It almost frightens me that people love her so much. I suppose that it is a good thing, and I hope that she will be worthy of it, poor little darling.'*

When Elizabeth was four-years-old, her younger sister Margaret Rose was born, however life for the elder Princess of York continued much as before. She developed a lifelong love of animals and, as she moved out of early childhood, it became clear that here was a very self-disciplined and conscientious little girl. She would put away her toys without having to be asked, fold up her clothes and always do as she was told. There was never any suggestion that Elizabeth attend school, her parents preferring to have her educated at home by a governess.

Elizabeth's fate changed forever in December 1936 when her Uncle David, now King Edward VIII, abdicated the throne to marry American divorcee Wallis Simpson, and her father became King George VI. Her father's coronation in Westminster Abbey in May 1937, had a profound effect on Elizabeth, now aged 11. She understood that one day, she too, would be crowned here. *'I thought it all very, very wonderful and I expect the Abbey did, too,'* she wrote. *'The arches and the beams at the top were covered with a sort of haze of wonder as Papa was crowned.'*

Left:
Princess Elizabeth of York and her younger sister Princess Margaret with gifts presented to them by members of the Disabled Soldier's Embroidery Society in 1933

The Princess Elizabeth

Now heir to the throne, Elizabeth received private tuition in constitutional history from the Vice-Provost of Eton College and learned French from a succession of governesses. In order for her to socialise with girls her own age, a Girl Guides company was set up at Buckingham Palace. *'We were all the daughters of Dukes so it wasn't at all democratic,'* one member remembered. Elizabeth's fellow guides were also expected to curtsey to her.

Although their main home was now Buckingham Palace, the family – *'we four'* as George VI liked to refer to himself, his wife and two daughters – preferred to spend as much time as possible at their favourite country home, Windsor Royal Lodge, where they enjoyed the simple pleasures of family life. However, this was no longer an option when, in September 1939, Britain went to war with Germany.

Politicians suggested that the two princesses be evacuated to Canada in order to avoid the aerial bombing but their mother refused to allow it. *'The children won't go without me. I won't leave without the King. And the King will never leave,'* she famously declared. Elizabeth and Margaret stayed at Balmoral Castle in Scotland until Christmas 1939 when they moved to Sandringham House, Norfolk. In May 1940, they relocated to Windsor Castle where they remained for much of the next five years. It was here that the princesses staged pantomimes at Christmas in aid of the Queen's Wool Fund, which purchased yarn to knit into military garments. In 1940, the 14-year-old Elizabeth made her first radio broadcast during the BBC's Children Hour in which she specifically addressed other children who had been evacuated from the cities. *'We are trying to do all we can to help our gallant sailors, soldiers and airmen, and we are trying, too, to bear our share of the danger and sadness of war,'* she stated. *'We know, every one of us, that in the end all will be well.'*

In 1943, Elizabeth undertook her first solo public appearance on a visit to the Grenadier Guards, of which she had been appointed colonel the previous year. As she approached her 18th birthday in April 1944, parliament changed the law so she could act as one of five Counsellors of State in the event of her father's incapacity or absence abroad, such as his visit to Italy in July 1944. In February 1945, she was appointed as an honorary second subaltern in the Auxiliary Territorial Service with the service number of 230873. She trained as a driver and mechanic and was given the rank of honorary junior commander after five months.

On Victory in Europe Day on May 8 1945, the princesses mingled anonymously with celebratory crowds on the streets of London. *'We asked my parents if we could go out and see for ourselves,'* Elizabeth later revealed in a rare interview. *'I remember we were terrified of being recognised ... I remember lines of unknown people linking arms and walking down Whitehall, all of us just swept along on a tide of happiness and relief.'*

In 1947, Princess Elizabeth went on her first overseas tour, accompanying her parents and sister through southern Africa. During the tour, in a broadcast on her 21st birthday, she made the following pledge: *'I declare before you all that my whole life, whether it be long or short, shall be devoted to your service and the service of our great Imperial family to which we all belong.'*

Unbeknown to everyone except her closest family, Elizabeth was determined to marry the man she had been in love with for eight years. In July 1939, the then 13-year-old had fallen for her third cousin, Prince Philip of Greece, the tall, blond 18-year-old tall midshipman who had been instructed to keep her and her little sister entertained while their parents toured the Royal Naval College in Dartmouth, Devon. During the war years, Elizabeth and Philip met occasionally whenever Philip's leave allowed. They corresponded as friends and the young princess kept a framed photo of Philip by her bed. When the war ended in May 1945, Elizabeth, now 19, was hopeful their friendship would develop into something more. Over that summer, the two met whenever possible and began to fall in love. A year later, on August 11 1946, 25-year-old Philip asked Elizabeth to marry him. She accepted immediately, even though her very protective father had not given them his permission. It was a secret engagement but word soon got out. Elizabeth was summoned by her parents who were worried about their young daughter marrying so worldly a man as Phillip. But Elizabeth was quietly determined to be with the man she had loved for so long. She stood up to her father saying that as her life would be one of duty to her country, surely she should be allowed to marry the man she loved. *'After all, you married Mummy,'* Elizabeth argued. *'She wasn't even Royalty – Philip is.'* Finally, a compromise was reached. The King would grudgingly consent to the engagement but it must remain secret while he, the Queen and the Princesses, toured South Africa. Elizabeth had no choice but to comply.

Once back in London and reunited, Elizabeth and Philip set about making plans. Having turned 21, the princess was now officially an adult and unwilling to wait any longer. On July 10 1947 – almost a year after Elizabeth had accepted Philip's clandestine proposal, the following announcement was made.

'It is with the greatest pleasure that the King and Queen announce the betrothal of their dearly beloved daughter the Princess Elizabeth to Lieutenant Philip Mountbatten RN . . . to which union the King has gladly given his consent.'

Above & Left:

H R H Princess Elizabeth and Philip Mountbatten, Duke of Edinburgh, on the occasion of their engagement at Buckingham Palace in London, July 1947

Right:

Princess Elizabeth and Prince Philip, Duke of Edinburgh at Buckingham Palace shortly before their wedding

As Royal Weddings go, Elizabeth and Philip's was not a grand affair as rationing was still in full force. The nuptials took place on November 20 1947 in Westminster Abbey and the bride had been granted 200 hundred extra clothing coupons for her bridal ensemble plus an extra 23 for each of her eight bridesmaids. Couturier Norman Hartnell, who had been making clothes for Queen Elizabeth and the princesses since the mid 1930s, was chosen to design the wedding dress – a stunning satin gown, embroidered in crystals and 10,000 costume pearls which had been sourced in the USA. The 15 feet train was decorated with white roses worked in padded satin, and sheaves of corn picked out in diamante and pearl embroidery.

Above:

The trumpeteers of the Royal Military School of Music rehearse for a fanfare to be played at Princess Elizabeth's wedding at Westminster Abbey. The fanfare has been specially composed by Sir Arnold Bax, Master of the King's Music

Left:

Princess Elizabeth & Prince Philip (front row center) posing with other family members as well as members of European nobility after their wedding, November 1947

Below:

Princess Elizabeth in the Irish State Coach accompanied by her father HM, King George VI passes huge crowds at Trafalgar Square, on her way to marry the Duke of Edinburgh at Westminster Abbey

After so many years of wartime austerity, London went wild with excitement

'The crowds were enormous,' one magazine reported. *'And it was a happy, good-tempered crowd obviously determined to enjoy its brief escape from what we have come to call austerity. Flags and streamers flowered from every hand and countless periscopes – most of them little mirrors fixed on pieces of stick – danced like crystallised sunshine above the tightly packed heads.'*

Before the marriage, Philip renounced his Greek and Danish titles, officially converting from Greek Orthodoxy to Anglicanism, and became Lieutenant Philip Mountbatten, taking the surname of his mother's British family. Just before the wedding, he was created His Royal Highness, The Duke of Edinburgh.
Less than a year after the marriage, Elizabeth gave birth to her first child, Prince Charles, on November 14 1948. A month earlier, the King had decreed that her children be allowed to use the style and title of a royal prince or princess, to which they otherwise would not have been entitled as their father was no longer a royal prince. Their second child, Princess Anne, was born in August 1950.

At various times between 1949 and 1951, the Duke of Edinburgh was stationed on the British Crown Colony of Malta as a serving Royal Navy officer. He and Elizabeth lived intermittently on the Mediterranean island during this time – their children remaining in the UK with their maternal grandparents. However, by 1951, George VI's health was declining, and Elizabeth frequently stood in for her ailing father at public events.

In early 1952, Elizabeth and Philip set out for a tour of Australia and New Zealand by way of Kenya. On February 6 1952, they had just returned to their Kenyan lodgings after a night spent at Treetops Hotel when word arrived of the death of the King. Elizabeth was now Queen Elizabeth II. Her secretary, Martin Charteris, asked Elizabeth, how, as Queen, she wished to be known.

'By my own name, of course,' she calmly replied. *'What else?'*

A new Elizabethan age had begun. . .

Above:
Princess Elizabeth with her husband, Prince Philip, and their children Prince Charles and the baby Princess Anne

Right:
Princess Elizabeth and the Duke of Edinburgh on honeymoon at Broadlands in Hampshire

Young Sovereign

Queen Elizabeth II, Coronation oath

'The things which I have here before promised, I will perform and keep. So help me God'

King George VI was laid to rest at St George's Chapel, Windsor on February 15 1952. However, he was barely cold in his grave before the new Queen had a potential constitutional crisis on her hands. Lord Louis Mountbatten, Prince Philip's uncle, had been witnessed at a dinner making a toast to the new reigning 'House of Mountbatten' - the presumption being that the reigning royal house would now bear Philip's name in line with the custom of a wife taking her husband's surname on marriage. The establishment - including the young Queen's mother and grandmother were firmly against the idea - and so that April, Elizabeth, possibly against her own personal desires - issued a declaration that Windsor would continue to be the name of the royal house. Philip was not happy.

Left:
The coronation of Elizabeth II took place on 2 June 1953 at Westminster Abbey in London

'I'm just a bloody amoeba,' he famously complained. *'I'm the only man in the country not allowed to give his name to his children.'*

It was a grievance that would rumble on for years but in a bid to placate her husband, Elizabeth insisted that Philip be given a high-profile role in the planning of her coronation – set for June 2 1953 - as Chair of the Coronation Commission. One of Philip's first recommendations was that the coronation be televised live and beamed into homes up and down the land, but this, too, caused controversy.

'It would be unfitting that the whole ceremony ... should be presented as if it were a theatrical performance,' said Prime Minister Winston Churchill. Others questioned whether broadcasting the event would be *'right and proper'*.

At the time no coronation had been televised before and attendance was typically reserved for the upper-classes. Elizabeth and the Queen Mother also voiced concerns about this unconventional suggestion but Philip's idea began to grow on his wife who was anxious to show the country she was its leader. Elizabeth, realizing that televising the coronation would be a way to break down class barriers, eventually decided she liked the idea. And so, after deliberation, those who were reluctant gave in. It was decided that the BBC would broadcast the event on live television although they would not be allowed to film the most sacred parts of the service, the anointing and the communion.

Elizabeth commissioned Norman Hartnell to create her coronation gown – as he had her white satin wedding gown six years earlier. Ordered in October 1952, the

Right:
4th June 1953: Queen Elizabeth II wearing a gown designed by Norman Hartnell for her Coronation ceremony

2nd June 1953. Coronation Day, the
Coronation of Queen Elizabeth II.
The Queen's coach just after
the crowning ceremony

Despite the death of Queen Mary on 24 March, the coronation went ahead as planned - as Mary had asked before she passed away. The day dawned dark and damp, and the huge crowds lining the London streets, many of whom had camped out over-night, were soaked through as they cheered the Queen and her Consort, travelling from Buckingham Palace to Westminster Abbey in the Gold State Coach, dating from the 1760s.

At 11.15am, the Queen processed from the west door of the Abbey, along the nave and choir, to the theatre that had been built at the east end. In her 250-strong procession, there were church leaders, Commonwealth prime ministers, members of the Royal Household, civil and military leaders, the Yeomen of the Guard and her six maids of honour, selected from the British aristocracy. Having knelt on the south side of the altar to pray privately before being 'recognised' with a rousing *'God save Queen Elizabeth'* from the congregation, Her Majesty then took the coronation oath, swearing to govern faithfully with justice and mercy, to uphold the Gospel, and to maintain the doctrine and worship of the Church of England. The Moderator of the General Assembly of the Church of Scotland presented the Queen with a Bible, *'To keep your Majesty ever mindful of the law and gospel of God as the rule for the whole life and government of Christian princes.'* Next came the Communion service. After the Creed, the Queen's crimson robe was removed, before she sat in the Coronation Chair, built by Edward I, to hold the Stone of Scone, taken from Scotland in 1296.

gown took eight months of research, design, workmanship and intricate embroidery to complete. Also made from white satin, it featured the floral emblems of the countries of the UK and those of other states within the Commonwealth of Nations. Encrusted with seed pearls, sequins and crystals, the designer added a secret detail for extra luck. Unbeknown to the Queen, Hartnell included an extra four-leaf shamrock on the left side of the skirt.

The Queen was now prepared for the religious and constitutional peak of the ceremony, the anointment – hidden from view – in which the Archbishop of Canterbury anointed the Queen with holy oil on her hands, breast and head. The oil was made from a secret mixture of ambergris, civet, orange flowers, roses, jasmine, cinnamon and musk. It was now that the Crown Jewels took centre stage. The holy oil was poured from Charles II's Ampulla, an eagle-shaped

Above:
The Crown Jewels - St Edward's Crown, the Orb, the Sceptre with Cross, Sceptre with Dove, and the Ring

Right: A programme for Queen Elizabeth II's coronation and a ticket for the stands erected along the route of the procession to the abbey through Piccadilly Circus

Far Right:
Queen Elizabeth II with The Prince Philip, Duke of Edinburgh looking out from her Coronation Coach en route to Westminster Abbey for the Coronation ceremony

THE CORONATION OF
HER MAJESTY
QUEEN ELIZABETH II

THE CEREMONIAL
2 JUNE 1953

The Coronation of Her Majesty
Queen Elizabeth II
TUESDAY 2 JUNE 1953

BLOCK
A

STAND
22

PICCADILLY

ROW   SEAT No.   PRICE
N   46   £4

ADMIT ONE

vessel, into a 12th-century spoon. Meanwhile, the choir sang 'Zadok the Priest' – the words, from the first Book of Kings, have been sung at every coronation since King Edgar's in 973. The anointment ritual is even older, going back to King Solomon, supposedly anointed by Zadok in the 10th century BC. Then the Queen was invested with her regalia. She was first given a pair of gold spurs (originally used for creating knights, when they literally earned their spurs), commissioned for the 1661 coronation of Charles II. Most of the Crown Jewels were made then, after the medieval regalia had been melted down in 1649 by the Commonwealth government.

The Queen received the sword of justice followed by the Sovereign's Orb. Representing Christ's authority over the globe, the spherical gold orb, circled by 365 rose-cut diamonds, was also made for Charles II's coronation. Once presented with the Sovereign's Ring, designed for William IV in 1831, the Queen then took up the sceptre with a cross – symbolising kingly power – and a rod, topped with a dove, symbolising justice and mercy. And then came the archetypal crowning moment, as the Archbishop placed St Edward's Crown – a 1661 imitation of its medieval predecessor – on the Queen's head, to trumpet fanfares and cries of *'God Save the Queen'* from the congregation. Several miles downstream, at the Tower of London, a gun salute was fired.

Once the benediction was over, the Queen moved from the Coronation Chair to the throne in the central part of the theatre. The enthronement was the moment at which she officially took possession of her kingdom, before receiving homage, first from the Archbishop of Canterbury, the bishops, the Duke of Edinburgh, and peers from the House of Lords. The service ended with the Queen receiving Holy Communion, before moving to St Edward's Chapel, where she put

Right:

Queen Elizabeth II seated upon the throne at her coronation in Westminster Abbey, London. She is holding the royal sceptre (ensign of kingly power and justice) and the rod with the dove (symbolising equity and mercy)

The newly crowned Queen Elizabeth II waves to the crowd
from the balcony at Buckingham Palace. Her children
Prince Charles and Princess Anne stand with her

on a purple velvet robe and swapped St Edward's Crown for the Imperial State Crown, designed in 1937 for George VI. As the National Anthem played, the Queen walked through the abbey past her subjects, sceptre and orb in her hands.

By 2pm, almost three hours after it began, the service was over, watched by 27 million people in the first ever coronation to be televised. After the parade back to Buckingham Palace, Elizabeth stood with her family on the balcony and waved to the crowd as jet planes of the Royal Air Force flew across the Mall in tight formation.

'Nothing was more memorable in the long solemnities than the manner in which Her Majesty bore her part in them. Not only at the Crowning but in every movement and gesture there was a deep sense of recollection. Dignity went hand in hand with modesty, simplicity with majesty, gravity with a charm which shone like crystal within all that glitter of imperial and ecclesiastical effulgence,' wrote The Times newspaper.

Post coronation, it was now the Queen's intention to focus on a lengthy tour of the Commonwealth. However, another family crisis took precedence which would, in retrospect, define the early years of this young sovereign's reign. Namely, the relationship between her younger sister,

---

Above:
The Sovereign's Orb

Right:
A portrait of young Elizabeth II (1926-) of Great Britain and Northern Ireland, wearing the crown of the kings and queens of England for her coronation in June of 1953

Princess Margaret, and their late father's trusted equerry, war hero Group Captain Peter Townsend. At the coronation, all eyes should have been on the new monarch. But someone else almost stole the show that afternoon. At the televised event, the queen's sister was witnessed picking a piece of lint from Townsend's jacket lapel and the intimate gesture sparked a royal scandal. Margaret's relationship with Townsend began in the early 1950s. Worldly, beautiful and charming, she was intensely attracted to the handsome veteran. But the formerly married Townsend was not considered an appropriate royal match. Though their affair was conducted in secret, the world soon learned that Group Captain Townsend had divorced his wife and proposed to Margaret— and that she had accepted.

At the time, divorce was considered a major scandal, and it was unthinkable for a royal to marry both a commoner and a divorced man. Since the Church of England looked down on the dissolution of marriage, Queen Elizabeth, head of the church as part of her duties as head of state, faced a considerable obstacle. If Margaret married Townsend, it might give the appearance that the Queen approved of divorce. There was another problem - the Royal Marriages Act of 1772. The law—which had its roots in George III's distaste for both of his brothers' marriages to commoners—gave the monarch ultimate say over who married whom. Under this act, all descendants of George II needed royal permission to marry. If they did not receive it, they could marry after one year of waiting as long as both houses of Parliament approved.

Margaret needed her sister's permission to marry Townsend. If she couldn't get it, she could beg Parliament for the right to marry, but that would have caused a scandal even more dramatic than her affair with a divorced man. Since the abdication of Edward VIII had rocked the royal family to its core less than 20 years earlier, this was unthinkable. The facts

seemed to make it impossible for Margaret to marry Townsend. Elizabeth asked her sister to wait for a year. Meanwhile, Parliament made it clear that they didn't support the match and as Head of the Church, which at the time did not allow divorced people to remarry, the Queen could not give her consent, either. However, Elizabeth had no wish to get in the way of her sister's happiness. Contrary to Netflix drama 'The Crown', which portrayed the Queen as ultimately blocking the marriage for the sake of the monarchy, the real-life Elizabeth did come around to the idea. She asked the couple to wait until Margaret turned 25 when she would no longer need the monarch's assent, although permission would still be necessary from the Government. Elizabeth even drew up a plan that would allow Margaret to marry Townsend and stay part of the family. The compromise would have amended the Royal Marriages Act and essentially made it unnecessary for the queen to give her permission at all. There was a catch, though - to marry

Townsend under this plan, Margaret would have had to give up her right of ever succeeding to the throne – likewise any children she may have in the future. It's not clear if this is why Margaret eventually broke off her relationship with Townsend, but the scandalous near-marriage never occurred.

'I would like it to be known that I have decided not to marry Group Capt. Peter Townsend,'

read her announcement on October 31 1955.

'Mindful of the church's teaching that Christian marriage is indissoluble, and conscious of my duty to the Commonwealth, I have resolved to put these considerations before any others.'

The Queen has never commented on her sister's decision but at the time, it no doubt came as a relief as it allowed the young monarch to give her all to the business of ruling. Something she has continued to do since the first day she ascended the throne.

Left:
Queen Elizabeth II and Prince Philip, Duke of Edinburgh. Coronation portrait, June 1953

Right:
Memorabilia from the 1953 coronation of Queen Elizabeth II

Family Matters

The Queen commenting on her brood

'Like all the best families, we have our share of eccentricities, of impetuous and wayward youngsters and of family disagreements'

The Queen is a mother of four, grandmother of eight, and great grandmother - at the time of writing - of 12. The Monarchy is - and always has been - very much a family affair. In addition to her direct descendants, Her Majesty is close to her paternal cousins - the Duke of Kent, Princess Alexandra and Prince Michael of Kent, and the Duke of Gloucester and his wife - some of whom, on occasion, are called on to represent the Queen. Every December - at least before the pandemic - Her Majesty hosts a Christmas lunch for the extended Royal Family, now thought to number at least 50 as the children and grandchildren of the Kent and Gloucester cousins are included.

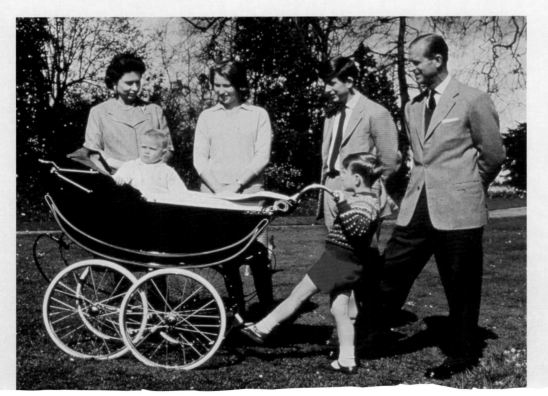

Left:
Queen Elizabeth II and The Prince Philip, Duke of Edinburgh with their children (right to left); Charles Prince of Wales, Prince Andrew, Prince Edward and Princess Anne celebrating the Queen's 39th birthday at Windsor in 1965

Family Matters

— 45 —

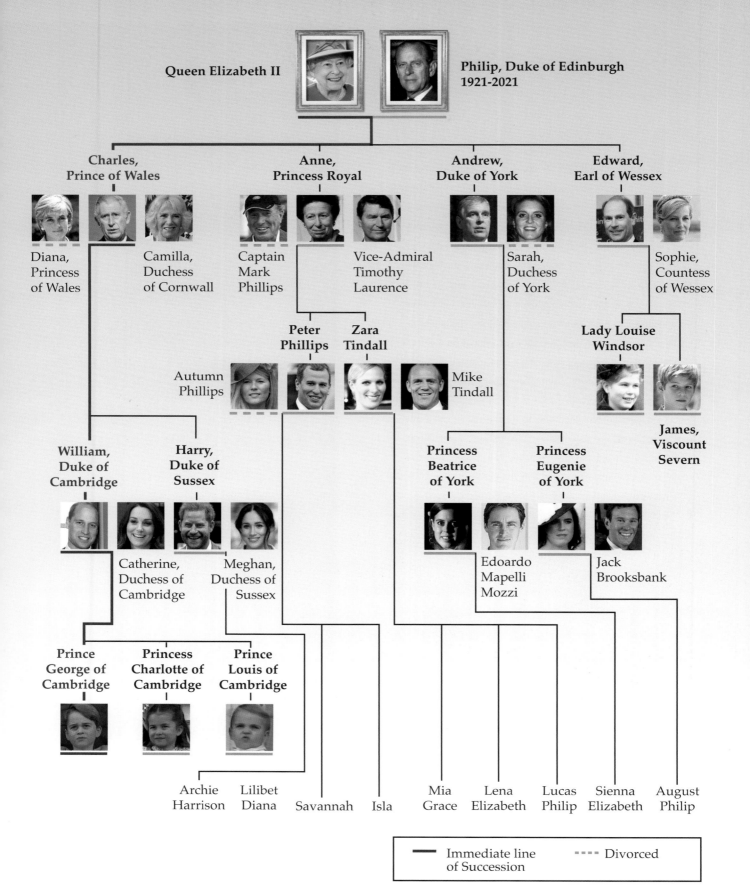

Queen Elizabeth II **Philip, Duke of Edinburgh**
1921-2021

Charles, **Anne,** **Andrew,** **Edward,**
Prince of Wales **Princess Royal** **Duke of York** **Earl of Wessex**

Diana, Camilla, Captain Vice-Admiral Sarah, Sophie,
Princess Duchess Mark Timothy Duchess Countess
of Wales of Cornwall Phillips Laurence of York of Wessex

Peter **Zara** **Lady Louise**
Phillips **Tindall** **Windsor**

Autumn Mike **James,**
Phillips Tindall **Viscount**
Severn

William, **Harry,** **Princess** **Princess**
Duke of **Duke of** **Beatrice** **Eugenie**
Cambridge **Sussex** **of York** **of York**

Catherine, Meghan, Edoardo Jack
Duchess of Duchess of Mapelli Brooksbank
Cambridge Sussex Mozzi

Prince **Princess** **Prince**
George of **Charlotte of** **Louis of**
Cambridge **Cambridge** **Cambridge**

Archie Lilibet Mia Lena Lucas Sienna August
Harrison Diana Savannah Isla Grace Elizabeth Philip Elizabeth Philip

| ——— Immediate line of Succession | - - - - Divorced |

The Queen's Immediate Descendants

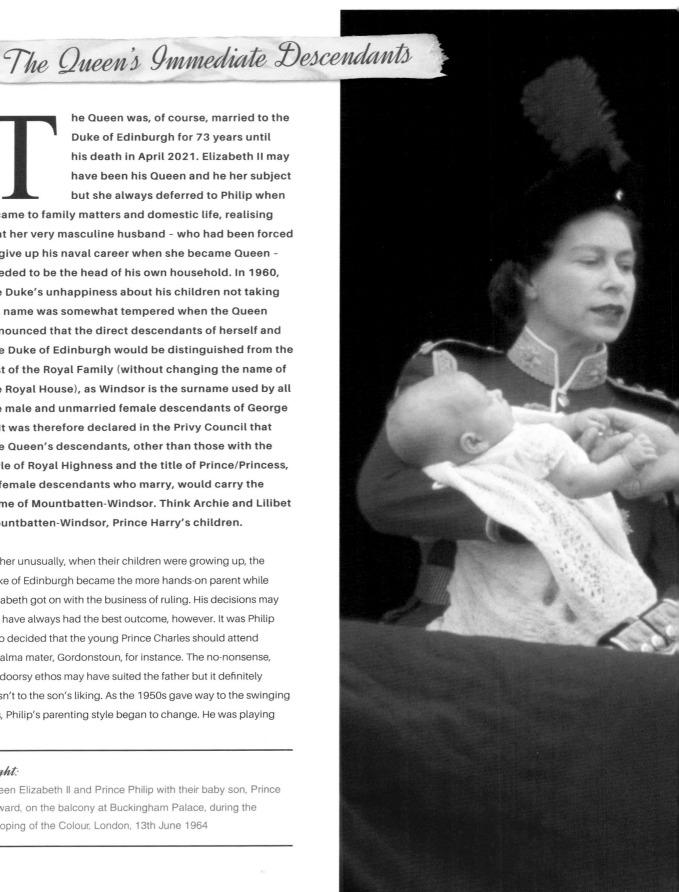

The Queen was, of course, married to the Duke of Edinburgh for 73 years until his death in April 2021. Elizabeth II may have been his Queen and he her subject but she always deferred to Philip when it came to family matters and domestic life, realising that her very masculine husband – who had been forced to give up his naval career when she became Queen – needed to be the head of his own household. In 1960, the Duke's unhappiness about his children not taking his name was somewhat tempered when the Queen announced that the direct descendants of herself and The Duke of Edinburgh would be distinguished from the rest of the Royal Family (without changing the name of the Royal House), as Windsor is the surname used by all the male and unmarried female descendants of George V. It was therefore declared in the Privy Council that The Queen's descendants, other than those with the style of Royal Highness and the title of Prince/Princess, or female descendants who marry, would carry the name of Mountbatten-Windsor. Think Archie and Lilibet Mountbatten-Windsor, Prince Harry's children.

Rather unusually, when their children were growing up, the Duke of Edinburgh became the more hands-on parent while Elizabeth got on with the business of ruling. His decisions may not have always had the best outcome, however. It was Philip who decided that the young Prince Charles should attend his alma mater, Gordonstoun, for instance. The no-nonsense, outdoorsy ethos may have suited the father but it definitely wasn't to the son's liking. As the 1950s gave way to the swinging 60s, Philip's parenting style began to change. He was playing

Right:

Queen Elizabeth II and Prince Philip with their baby son, Prince Edward, on the balcony at Buckingham Palace, during the Trooping of the Colour, London, 13th June 1964

squash when Elizabeth gave birth to Charles in 1948 but was with his wife throughout her labour when Edward arrived 16 years later. Together, Elizabeth and Philip experienced more than 73 years of state visits, ceremonies and charitable initiatives, family milestones both good and bad, and a mounting tally of grandchildren and then great-grandchildren. There were countless summers spent at Balmoral, Christmases at Sandringham, and voyages on the royal yacht Britannia that, until she was decommissioned in 1997, was perhaps the couple's most personal home. During picnics at Balmoral, Philip would be manning the barbeque as head chef while the Queen was his assistant and the washer-upper. Looking back on the occasion of their Golden Wedding anniversary in 1997, speaking at the Guildhall the day before his wife made her own laudatory speech, Prince Philip remarked that time seems to fly when you are busy – and that to he and his wife, the previous 50 years had indeed seemed busy. Prince Philip had been patron of

some 850 organisations, more even than are sponsored by the Queen, as well as managing the family's estates.

'It's been a challenge for us but, by trial and experience, I believe we have achieved a sensible division of labour and a good balance between our individual and joint interests,' he declared.

The following day his wife declared that *'I, and his whole family, and this and many other countries, owe him a debt greater than*

Above:

Elizabeth II with her son Prince Andrew in a pram and Princess Anne September 1960

Right:

New born Prince Andrew in Queen Elizabeth II's arms

he would ever claim, or we shall ever know. My husband has quite simply been my strength and stay all these years.'

As the years rolled by, the companionship within their long marriage became ever more important – especially after the Queen lost her beloved mother and sister, Margaret, within weeks of each other in 2002. Although the Queen was said to have been prepared for Philip's demise after months of him suffering from ill health, she was grief-stricken by his passing. The image of her sitting alone at his funeral at St George's Chapel, Windsor, sums this up better than words ever could.

For Charles, Anne, Andrew, and Edward, sharing a mother with the nation and the Commonwealth was simply a reality growing up. But there were complications – for uber-sensitive Charles, in particular. When Queen Elizabeth II had Charles and Anne, she was in her 20s and engaging in intense trial-by-fire training, meaning she had to place Crown and Country above all else. But for Andrew and Edward - born more than 10 years later - the Queen had finally relaxed into her role as monarch and was able to actually enjoy being a mother. She took a full 18 months off after Andrew's birth and enjoyed taking care of him herself, a luxury she didn't have with Charles and Anne. It was a similar length of maternity leave when Edward, after a difficult pregnancy, was born in 1964. Throughout her reign, the Queen has frequently taken long trips to foreign countries, but none more controversial

than the punishing six-month tour of the Commonwealth she – and Philip - embarked on in 1953 without Charles, then six, or Anne, three. Although the young Queen was thrilled to be a mother, Prince Charles has said that the nursery staff brought him up, teaching him to play, punishing and rewarding him, and

even watching his first steps. Times were different then, however, and the Queen was simply recreating how she herself had been raised. Her parents, King George VI and Queen Elizabeth, had frequently entrusted her and sister Margaret to nannies and governesses. Even when Elizabeth and Philip were home, it was usual for them to only see the children after breakfast and teatime. For Charles his mother was *'not indifferent so much as detached'*. However gung-ho Anne took a different view.

'We as children may have not been too demanding in the sense that we understand what the limitations were in time and the responsibilities placed on her as monarch in the things she had to do and the travels she had to make,' said the Princess Royal in 2002. *'But I don't believe any of us for a second thought she didn't care for us in exactly the same way as any other mother did."*

Left:
Queen Elizabeth II and Prince Philip, Duke of Edinburgh and their children at Windsor on the Queen's 39th birthday, April 1965

Above:
The two youngest children of Queen Elizabeth, Prince Andrew, left, and baby, Prince Edward

When actress Kate Winslet was awarded the honour of a CBE at Buckingham Palace in 2012, she and the Queen discussed motherhood. Elizabeth asked the Academy Award-winning actress if she liked her job, and Winslet—a mother of two children at the time—replied yes, adding, *'But I love being a mum even more'*. Incredibly, considering her position as arguably the most famous and influential woman in the world, the Queen agreed. *'Yes,'* Her Majesty replied. *'It is the best job.'*

Certainly, her former daughter-in-law, Sarah Ferguson, sees the Queen as the ultimate mother figure.

'I think to myself that honestly, my mother-in-law has been more of a mother to me than my mother,' she has said. *'I absolutely admire the incredible way Her Majesty is so modern. And how flexible, and how understanding, and how forgiving and how generous. I absolutely think there is no greater mentor. The consistency of Her Majesty has been a great honour. A huge honour and it makes me want to cry.'*

Right:
The Queen and Prince Philip with their four children in 1965

Below:
Queen Elizabeth, the Queen Mother (1900-2002) sits with her grandchildren Prince Charles, Princess Anne and baby Prince Andrew

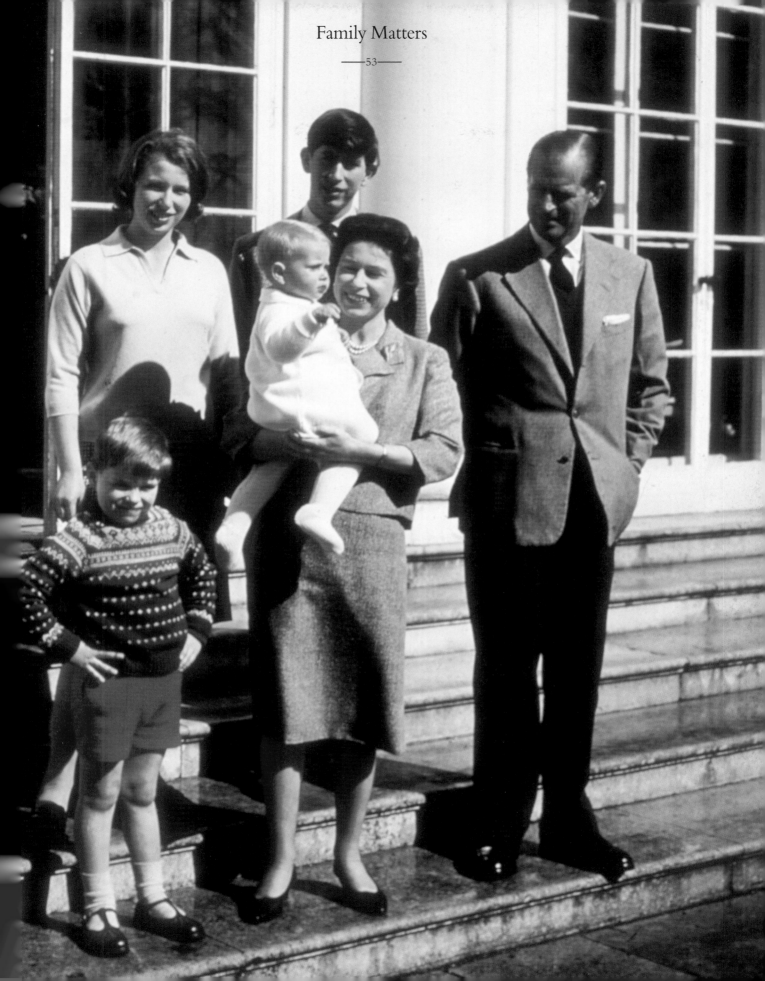

Above:
Surrounded by Royal relatives and godparents who are amused at the antics of young Prince William, Prince Harry is christened at Windsor Castle on December 21, 1984

Left:
Princess Diana cuddling her baby son, Prince Harry, aboard the Royal Yacht Britannia during her tour of Italy in May 1985

The Queen became a grandmother for the first time when Princess Anne gave birth to a son, Peter Phillips, in November 1977. Like most grannies, this Royal one was totally smitten with the new arrival. Indeed, for one of the first times ever, the Queen was late for an investiture – delayed by telephoning her husband, who was in Germany, to tell him the news. Arriving at the investiture, she momentarily forgot to ask her guests to sit down.

'I apologise for being late,' she said, her face all-smiles, *'but I have just had a message from the hospital. My daughter has just given birth to a son.'*

The arrival of a further seven grandchildren – Zara Phillips in May 1981, Prince William in June 1982, Prince Harry in September 1984, Princess Beatrice of York in August 1988, Princess Eugenie

of York in April 1990, Lady Louise Mountbatten Windsor in November 2003 and James Viscount Severn in December 2007 – were greeted just as enthusiastically. Known as *'Gary'* until the toddler Prince William could pronounce Granny, the Queen has always been the ultimate role model for this future King.

Above:
Prince William & Diana pose for portraits in the sitting room of their home in Kensington Palace

Left:
Prince William giggles with his hand over his mouth as he and baby brother, Harry, pretended to play the piano during a private photo session at home in Kensington Palace

Right:
Prince Charles laughing with his sons as he lifts Prince Harry onto Prince William's shoulders in Kensington Palace

---

'Growing up, having this figurehead, having this stability above me has been incredible,' he said. 'I have been able to explore, understand, slightly carve my own path. I greatly appreciate and value that protection.'

She is known to be a loving and interested granny to all eight grandchildren. Protective, too. As the first marriages of Charles and Anne, and also the marriage of Andrew to Sarah Ferguson fell apart, she was most concerned about the welfare of her grandchildren. And who can forget that it was in order to protect Princes William and Harry – as their grandmother – that she insisted on remaining in Balmoral with the boys after the tragic death of their mother on August 31 1997? On a happier note, Her Majesty loaned grand-daughters Zara, Beatrice and Eugenie, and grand-daughters-in-law Catherine and Megan, fabulous tiaras on their wedding days – in addition to allowing Beatrice to wear one of her vintage gowns as a bridal gown in 2020. These days she is said to be especially close to her two youngest grandchildren, Louise and James, the children of the Earl and Countess of Wessex. Lady Louise, 18, is thought to regularly visit her grandmother at both Windsor and Balmoral, and is rumoured to have a very down to earth bond with Her Majesty. So normal, in fact, is the Wessex children's relationship with the monarch, that Lady Louise spent years in the dark about who her grandmother really was.

Speaking in an interview recorded ahead of Her Majesty's 90th birthday in 2016, the Countess of Wessex told Sky News, 'I mean Louise had no concept really that the Queen and her grand-mother were one and the same person. It wasn't until she was at school that other children were mentioning it and saying, "Your gran is the Queen". And she'd come home and say, "Mummy they say that Grandmama is the Queen". And I said, "Yes" and she said, "I don't understand what they mean".'

Louise clearly takes after her father. Prince Edward has said he didn't realise his mother was monarch until he was five or six.

Known as Gan-Gan to her great grandchildren, Her Majesty is, according to her granddaughter-in-law, the Duchess of Cambridge, very kind, loving and thoughtful towards her grandchildren's off-spring.

'Every time we stay with her, she leaves a little gift for George and Charlotte in their rooms, and that just shows her love for her family,' Kate revealed in 2016.

However, in the Royal Family, manners are a must — and the Queen is more than happy to teach her great-grandchildren how to be respectful. While visiting at Buckingham Palace, Prince George was told by his great grandmother to tidy away his toys as it was not the job of the staff to do it.

Go Gan-Gan.

Above:

Prince William, Duke of Cambridge and Catherine, Duchess of Cambridge depart the Lindo Wing at St Mary's Hospital with their new born son Prince George on July 22, 2013

Left:

Catherine, Duchess of Cambridge and Prince William, Duke of Cambridge depart the Lindo Wing, St Mary's Hospital with their new born daughter Princess Charlotte on May 2, 2015

Above:
The Duchess of Cambridge and Prince George attend the Jerudong Park Trophy at Cirencester Park Polo Club on June 15, 2014

Left:
Duchess of Cambridge and Princess Charlotte at a children's party for Military families during the Royal Tour of Canada on September 29, 2016

Right:
Catherine, Duchess of Cambridge, Princess Charlotte of Cambridge and Prince George of Cambridge, Prince William, Duke of Cambridge at a children's party for Military families during the Royal Tour of Canada on September 29, 2016 in Victoria, Canada

Queen, Commonwealth and Country

Queen Elizabeth II

'I cannot lead you into battle. I do not give you laws or administer justice but I can do something else — I can give my heart and my devotion to these old islands and to all the peoples of our brotherhood of nations'

Elizabeth's commitment to the Commonwealth has been plain to see from the very beginning of her very long reign. Her first tour of these territories began in November 24 1953 and lasted six months. She and the Duke of Edinburgh covered a massive distance of 43,618 miles as they visited Canada, Bermuda, Jamaica, Panama, Tonga, New Zealand, Australia - where they stayed for 58 days, the Cocos Islands, Ceylon (now Sri Lanka), Aden, Uganda, Libya, Malta and Gibraltar. Her 1953 Christmas broadcast that year was recorded in Auckland in New Zealand.

Right:
The Queen and the Duke of Edinburgh visiting Bermuda in 1953

'I set out on this journey in order to see as much as possible of the people and countries of the Commonwealth and Empire,' she said. *'I want to show that the Crown is not merely an abstract symbol of our unity but a personal and living bond between you and me.'*

In the years since, she has completed 200 tours of Commonwealth countries – either singly such as her visit to India in 1983 or as part of a countries-wide itinerary. She has visited 28 Commonwealth nations - with the exception of Cameroon which joined in 1995 and Rwanda which joined in 2009 - and has made many repeat visits. The Commonwealth Country she has visited the most is Canada (27 visits), followed by Australia (18) and New Zealand (10). But the Queen hasn't neglected the smaller members of the Commonwealth family. The

Above:
A young girl presenting flowers to The Queen outside Brisbane City Hall, March 1954

Queen Elizabeth II is greeted by a young girl at an official welcome at a quayside in Fiji during the coronation world tour, December 1953. Behind the queen are the Governor of Fiji, Sir Ronald Garvey (1903 - 1991, in plumed helmet) and Prince Philip

Above Left:
The Queen cutting a cake in celebration of the first birthday of Prince Andrew in Chennai, India, 19 February 1961

Above Right:
The Queen and the Duke of Edinburgh in Sydney, Australia, February 1963

Left:
The Queen with Brian Elwood, Mayor of Palmerston North, New Zealand, during a walkabout in The Square, 26 February 1977

Right:
The Queen and the Duke of Edinburgh at the opening of the New Zealand Parliament in 1963

tiny island nation of Nauru is not an easy place to visit. With 11,000 people living on its eight-square miles, Nauru in the Pacific Ocean is the world's smallest island country. And yet, had you gone there in October 1982, you would have seen a beaming Queen Elizabeth in a blue and white dress meeting children on the dockside. Nauru joined the Commonwealth in 1968 and the Queen decided this country, like many other member states, deserved a visit from the organisation's head. Her tours were not all about world leaders and big summits but primarily about people. And the Queen - who once said *'I have to be seen to be believed'* - chose to travel, where possible, in the most visually accessible way. Not just open-top cars and jeeps but sometimes by canoe! In Tuvalu in 1982, for example, she was carried aloft in a war canoe through the streets of one of the coral atolls that make up the South Pacific nation.

'I always felt that the Queen enjoys travel,' says Charles Anson, who accompanied the Queen abroad as her Press Secretary during the 1990s. *'She is genuinely curious about people, their different cultures, traditions and quirks.'*

It was in fact on an overseas tour to Australia and New Zealand in 1970 that Her Majesty instigated a tradition of her own – the Royal Walkabout. The practice was introduced to allow the Queen and the Duke of Edinburgh to meet a greater number of people, not simply officials and dignitaries.

A deeply significant Commonwealth visit came at a meeting with Nelson Mandela at a Commonwealth heads of government summit in 1991 in South Africa, a year after his release from

prison. He would not become the country's president until 1994, but the Queen's relationship with Mandela – some say it was better described as a friendship – began with a mix-up at the formal banquet for the Commonwealth leaders. Mandela was not on the guest list as he wasn't a head of government at the time,

Above:
Queen Elizabeth meets Nelson Mandela in Cape Town during her trip to South Africa, March 25, 1995

but the Queen decided he should be at the dinner anyway.

According to Anson, *'they clicked right away'* because they both shared a deeply held belief that societies should be multiracial. The former press secretary adds: *'I remember they talked about the way international sport, and the televising of it, had helped to break down barriers between people of different races all over the world.'*

In fact, the relationship between the two was so warm, Mandela could say things other leaders couldn't.

'He was the only leader whom I recall sometimes calling the Queen by her first name in private conversations,' recalls Anson. *'And it seemed totally natural.'*

The Queen returned to South Africa in 1995 as a guest of President Mandela, and he was invited to Buckingham Palace the following year. For a Queen who has steadfastly avoided politics all her life, she has had quite an influence on the world's politicians. When another African leader, Kwame Nkrumah of Ghana, wanted to leave the Commonwealth in 1961 in favour of stronger ties with the Soviet Union, she visited despite the threat of bombs in the capital. Not only did she visit but she also danced. The tour provided one of the most memorable images of all - the Queen foxtrotting with President Nkrumah at a ball in Accra. The President kept Ghana in the Commonwealth. The late Kenneth Kaunda, President of Zambia from 1964-91, was quoted as saying that the transition from Empire to Commonwealth had only been made possible by the Queen's personality.

'Without that,' he remarked, *'many of us would have left.'*

While one third of the Queen's overseas visits have been to Commonwealth nations, there have also been many tours and state visits to other countries. She has, for instance, visited the USA in an official capacity on six occasions and - either in the US or on state visits to the UK – has met all American Presidents since Harry Truman. She is the only British monarch in history to have visited Russia – Her Majesty and the Duke of Edinburgh were hosted by President Putin on a state visit in 1994, and in 1986 she became the first British sovereign to go to China.

The most well-known royal photographer of recent times, Arthur Edwards of The Sun newspaper, has looked through his lens many times as the Queen travelled the world to meet leaders of state and church alike. He recalls the moment at the Vatican in 2000 when the Queen, Defender of the Faith and Supreme Governor of the Church of England, met Pope John Paul II, the leader of the worldwide Catholic Church. It wasn't their first meeting – they'd met twice in the 1980s – but on this occasion the pontiff was frail and struggled to talk.

'The Queen took complete control of the situation,' Edwards remembers. *'The Pope's words were barely audible but she repeated them loudly so we could all hear them.'*

Elizabeth II's visit to the Irish Republic in 2011 will also be remembered for many years to come. It was the first visit by a reigning monarch since George V – Elizabeth's grandfather – had visited what was then still part of the British Isles 100 years earlier.

'A Uachtaráin agus a chairde,' she said in Gaelic at the start of her speech in Dublin Castle, which translates as *'President and friends...'* It was a gesture of reconciliation that went a very long way. The Queen then added, *'With the benefit of historical hindsight we can all see things which we would wish had been done differently or not at all.'*

The day before she had stood next to the President of Ireland, Mary McAleese, and the two women laid wreaths at the Garden of Remembrance where Ireland honours those killed fighting against the British.

'The Queen is perhaps the best example of soft power at work,' says Anson.

Arthur Edwards, who was also in Dublin that night, remembers the tour well.

'It gave me goose bumps that one,' he says. *'It's the best visit I've ever done with the Queen and you could almost feel the two countries move forward in that moment.'*

Elizabeth II has become a much loved and respected figure across the globe. Her extraordinary reign has seen her travel more widely than any other monarch. When she gave up overseas travel, aged 89, after visiting Malta in 2015, she had flown the equivalent of 42 times around the globe – 1,032,513 miles in total - and visited 117 different countries.

At home in the UK, Her Majesty is no less dedicated. She regards her position as a sacred duty rather than an honour or privilege, and has remains as committed to her role as she was when she ascended the throne. Well into her ninth decade she was still undertaking 400-plus engagements a year – in person and then remotely by computer once the pandemic hit – and it was only after she had been advised by doctors to cut back on work in 2021 that she reluctantly agreed to do so. The Queen sees public and voluntary service as one of the most important elements of her duties and has links - as Royal Patron or President - with over 600 charities, military associations, professional bodies and public service organisations. These vary from well-established international charities to smaller bodies working in a specialist area or on a local basis only. Her patronages and charities cover a wide range of issues, from opportunities for young people to the preservation of wildlife and the environment. Having Her Majesty as Royal patron or president provides vital publicity for the work of these organisations, and allows their enormous achievements and contributions to society to be recognised.

Every day of the year, apart from Christmas Day, sees the Queen working from papers delivered to her in a famous red box. These boxes contain documents she receives from government ministers and from her representatives in Commonwealth and foreign countries. These include Cabinet documents, Foreign Office correspondence, a daily summary of events in Parliament, letters and other State papers, which have to be read and, where necessary, approved and signed. She still uses the boxes made for her on her coronation, embossed with the words *'The Queen'*

which have been refurbished over the years. She also scans newspapers and reviews her correspondence which amounts to 200-300 letters a day!

'She is very assiduous and careful about reading things and when you discussed things with her, she had read them very carefully,' a former deputy private secretary has remarked. *'You don't very often get a question or comment. But you know it's all sinking in and almost certainly some of it gets played back when she meets the prime minister at her weekly meeting or has audiences with new ambassadors.'*

The passage of a year in the life of every nation is marked in many different ways, some palpable - like the natural seasons - some which stem from ancient tradition - such as religious festivals - and others which take root around great sporting occasions. In the United Kingdom, the sovereign's annual calendar defines the nation's calendar, with its moments of high ceremony such as the Royal Maundy Service at Easter, Trooping the Colour and Ascot in June, the famous garden parties at Buckingham Palace and Holyrood House in July, the Highland Games in Scotland in August, and the State Opening of Parliament and the Service of Remembrance in the Autumn. Investitures, lunches, receptions, state visits and banquets take place alongside these set-in-stone events and nationwide engagements throughout the year. During the Queen's reign each month of the year has come to have its own cycle of events, and each royal residence its own season or month of heightened activity. The aim has always been to ensure that Her Majesty's duties as Head of State and Head of Nations are discharged in ways that are visible, tangible and relevant to the lives of as many people as possible.

Left:
The Queen, the Duke of Edinburgh, Prince Andrew, Prince Edward at the opening of the 1978 Commonwealth Games in Edmonton, Alberta

Right:
The Queen, the Duke of Edinburgh and Princess Anne during the 1970 Royal tour of Australia

Above:
Queen Elizabeth II and Prince Philip leave after a meeting
with Pope John Paul II at his private library in the Apostolic
Palace on October 17, 2000 in Vatican City, Vatican

The Worst of Times

The Queen's speech on the 40th anniversary of her succession to the throne

'1992 is not a year on which I shall look back with undiluted pleasure'

While Her Majesty may live in the ultimate lap of luxury and want for nothing, this is no guarantee against life's hardships. Anything but. In fact, her exalted position and role as constitutional monarch have thrown up many, many problems in the course of her 70-year reign.

Above:
Lord Altrincham in 1957

Right:
TV Times cover featuring Queen Elizabeth II, circa December 1955

The 1950s

We have already touched on the issue of her sister Margaret's controversial relationship with Group Captain Peter Townsend in the early days of the Queen's reign. But less than 12 months after that crisis passed in 1956, Elizabeth was having to face criticism about the very way she ruled. In August 1957, Lord Altrincham, in his publication 'The National and English Review' attacked the Queen in what amounted to a character assassination. He called her style of speaking a *'pain in the neck'* - adding that, *'The personality conveyed by the utterances which are put into her mouth is that of a priggish schoolgirl, captain of the hockey team, a prefect, and a recent candidate for Confirmation.'* According to the article, the Queen's court was too upper-class, too British and no longer reflected 20th century society, and this was damaging the monarchy.

While the majority of the mainstream press were outraged by these comments, on opposite sides of the political spectrum, the New Statesman and The Spectator agreed with some of Altrincham's opinions. It's not known whether Her Majesty was greatly upset by this dissent but it certainly seems like she took the criticisms to heart. Changes did take place following Lord Altrincham's article. The Queen made her first televised Christmas Message that year, telling her subjects that she wanted them to feel closer to her as their sovereign. She also sought to change the image of royalty - for example, the traditional 'presentation parties' for young upper-class debutantes at court were replaced by more accessible 'garden parties' which included a broader range of people.

It was also during this decade that rumours started to circulate about the state of Her Majesty's marriage. Some of Philip's activities, like his gentleman's lunch club and the solo tours he took throughout the 1950s on the royal yacht Britannia, led to speculation about possible infidelities. In 1957, 'The Baltimore Sun' carried a story that said he was *'romantically involved with an unnamed woman whom he met on a regular basis in the West End apartment of a society photographer.'* The palace followed this report with a denial - *'It is quite untrue that there is any rift between the Queen and the Duke.'* Philip once addressed the logistics of his conducting affairs, asking, *'How could I? I've had a detective in my company, night and day, since 1947.'* But some quarters have alluded to the fact that from the 1950s onwards, the Duke learned to carry on his flirtations and relationships in circles rich and grand enough to provide protection from the paparazzi and the tabloids. Whatever the truth of the matter, by 1959 the Royal marriage was clearly back on track. In February 1960, Her Majesty gave birth to Prince Andrew.

Below:
The royal yacht Britannia in 1959

The 1960s

While domestic life seemed harmonious enough for the Queen throughout these years, in 1966 disaster struck when, on October 21, a tsunami of black sludge rushed from the hill above the Welsh mining town of Aberfan, engulfing entire buildings and destroying everything in its wake. Over 140,000 cubic yards of coal waste from the mine fell that day, killing 144 people—most of them children whose classrooms were in the path of the runoff. Television crews captured a village in mourning, and an outpouring of support for the families of Aberfan rippled across the country. While the Queen was made aware of the tragedy shortly after it happened, she waited eight days to visit the Welsh community, a delay, which she is still said to regret immensely.

'Aberfan affected the Queen very deeply, I think, when she went there. It was one of the few occasions in which she shed tears in public,' said Sir William Heseltine, who served in the royal press office at the time. *'I think she felt in hindsight that she might have gone there a little earlier. It was a sort of lesson for us that you need to show sympathy and to be there on the spot, which I think people craved from her.'*

It seems this wasn't a decision made out of coldness, but rather practicality.

'People will be looking after me,' she is thought to have said. *'Perhaps they'll miss some poor child that might have been found under the wreckage.'*

Despite numerous suggestions that she should make the trip as soon as was possible, the Queen didn't change her mind.

'We kept presenting the arguments,' said a royal advisor, *'but nothing we said could persuade her.'*

Right:
The Queen and Prince Philip visiting Aberfan. 29th October 1966

The 1970s

The Queen had breathed a sigh of relief when her younger sister Margaret married society photographer Anthony Armstrong Jones in 1960 but 10 years on, the marriage was decidedly shaky with infidelities on both sides. In 1976, a tabloid British newspaper published photographs of Princess Margaret swimming off the coast of the private island of Mustique with a man 17 years her junior - 28-year-old Roddy Llewellyn, a landscape gardener, aristocrat...and her lover. The tabloids attacked Margaret for spending the public's money partying and portrayed Llewellyn as her 'toy boy'. Though her husband, who travelled often for his work as a photographer, had been having multiple affairs out in the open, it was Princess Margaret who was censured. Shortly after the publication of the photos, Snowden moved out of the family home at Kensington Palace. It was announced that the couple had mutually agreed to live apart.

'The Queen is naturally very sad at what happened,' said her press secretary at the time, adding that there had been no pressure from Her Majesty on either Margaret or Snowden to take any particular course of action. Perhaps not but once the photos of Margaret and Roddy had been made public, thus impinging on the image of the monarchy, Elizabeth was forced to act. Having lived apart for two years, Prince Margaret and her husband quietly divorced in 1978.

A year later, the Queen and her family were shocked to the core when on August 27 1979, the IRA detonated a bomb planted in Lord Louis Mountbatten's fishing boat as his family left on a fishing trip from Mullaghmore Harbour on the West Coast of Ireland. 'Uncle Dickie', aged 78, was killed instantly. His death affected Elizabeth greatly – not least because Dickie had been a great help when it came to communicating with Prince Charles.

Below:

Killing of Lord Louis Mountbatten by IRA explosion at Mullaghmore, Co. Sligo. Canon T. S. Wood, Church of Ireland Chaplin at Sligo General Hospital, with Bobby Molloy, Ray MacSharry and Denis Gallagher, TD at the removal of the bodies from Sligo General Hospital, Circa August 1979

The 1980s

Despite having to deal with an intruder in her bedroom at Buckingham Palace in 1982 and the worries she felt as a mother when son Andrew went to war in the Falklands that same year, in retrospect the 1980s were, for the Queen, a lull before the storm of the 1990s. Daughter Anne gave birth to her second child Zara in May 1981, and son and heir Charles married Lady Diana Spencer two months later – infecting the nation, if not the world, with Royal Wedding fever. The accession was assured when Diana gave birth to Prince William of Wales on June 21 1982. Prince Harry followed in September 1984. In July 1986, second son Prince Andrew married Sarah Ferguson and their daughter Beatrice arrived two years later. On the surface, all seemed well with the Windsors'. It was anything but. . .

Right:
Michael Fagan, the intruder who gained access to the bedroom of Queen Elizabeth II in Buckingham Palace in 1982, pictured at the entrance to the Tower of London in 1985

Below:
On 4 May 1982, two days after the sinking of General Belgrano, the British lost the Type 42 destroyer HMS Sheffield to fire following an Exocet missile strike from the Argentine 2nd Naval Air Fighter/Attack Squadron

The 1990s

This was the decade that would prove the most testing for the Queen – until the 2020s at any rate. She had to deal with the breakdown of three of her children's marriages. Anne's 19-year union with Captain Mark Phillips ended relatively quietly in April 1992. But not so the marriages of Charles and Andrew.

By 1992, the marriage between Prince Andrew and Sarah Ferguson was faltering. The Duchess was linked with various men including Texan multimillionaire Steve Wyatt, while her husband was away on royal duties. They agreed to separate in March 1992, however seven months later, paparazzi photos published in British tabloid 'The Daily Mirror' showed a topless, sunbathing Sarah and American financial advisor, John Bryan, apparently in the act of sucking her toes. Sarah was staying at Balmoral with the Queen and other members of the Royal Family when the photos emerged in the press.

'She was at Balmoral when those photographs came out,' says royal biographer, Penny Junor. 'The family came down for breakfast and there was Fergie in this shocking scene and that was the end.'

The ending of the Prince and Princess of Wales marriage was even more catastrophic. The relationship had been in decline for several years but it was in 1992 that recordings of Diana's phone conversations with her friend and lover James Gilbey were leaked. The release of the recordings was dubbed 'Squidgygate' by the press, as Gilbey called Diana 'Squidgy' in addition to 'darling' throughout the calls. Later that year, intimate calls between Charles and Camilla - otherwise known as 'Camillagate'. Diana and Charles' marital problems escalated with the publication of Andrew Morton's book 'Diana: Her True Story'. The book detailed Diana's loveless marriage, Charles' affairs, and the Princess' own struggles with bulimia, self-harm, and suicidal thoughts. By the end of the year, Charles and Diana's marriage was dissolved with British Prime Minister John Major formally announcing their separation.

'The Queen was grey and ashen and completely flat,' remembers one courtier. 'She looked so awful, I felt like crying.'

It was also in 1992 – on November 20 - that Windsor Castle caught fire, spreading through 100 rooms, destroying St George's Hall and a number of state rooms in its path. It seemed like a powerful symbol of the Windsor's year from hell. In news' footage, Her Majesty looked a forlorn, lonely figure - misery and sadness etched on her tired face. It was just four days after the inferno that she made her 'Annus Horribilis' speech at the Guildhall in London.

Happily, Windsor Castle would, in time, be restored – financed by opening Buckingham Palace to the paying public during the summer months. Sadly, the same could not be said for the Wales' marriage. A year and a half after their separation, Prince Charles gave a bombshell television interview where he admitted to infidelity. That night, Diana attended a party at London's Serpentine Gallery, wearing none other than the so-called 'revenge dress'. Tension within the family peaked when Diana gave an in-depth interview on the BBC programme, 'Panorama'. The Princess spoke about her struggles with bulimia, self-harm, and depression. She admitted her own adultery and expressed doubts about Charles' capacity to be King. She also spoke at length about Charles' affair with Camilla. Once regarded as unthinkable, now divorce was the only option – and the sooner the better.

'I have consulted with the Archbishop of Canterbury and with the Prime Minister and, of course, with Charles,'

she wrote in a curt letter to Diana,

'and we have decided that the best course for you is divorce.'

The divorce was finalised in 1996. Just a year later, on August 31 1997, Diana was tragically killed in a car accident in Paris.

Right:
Aerial view of Windsor Castle 3 days after the fire

Left:

Prince William, Prince of Wales, with his sons Princes William and Harry looking at floral tributes left at Kensington Palace following the death of Diana, Princess of Wales in September, 1997

The Queen wanted a private, 'no fuss' funeral in accordance with Diana's status as a private person. But Her Majesty had seriously misjudged the public's love for Diana as flowers piled up outside her London home, Kensington Palace, and mass grief swept Britain and the world. The Royal Family remained silent amid growing public anger and the Queen was widely criticised for not flying the flag at half-mast at Buckingham Palace. For perhaps the first time in her life, the people were not on the Queen's side. Finally, on Friday, September 5, the eve of Diana's funeral — and at the urging of then-prime minister Tony Blair and Prince Charles — the Queen made a live broadcast from Buckingham Palace *as your Queen and as a grandmother'.*

'I want to pay tribute to Diana myself,' she said. *'She was an exceptional and gifted human being. In good times and bad, she never lost her capacity to smile and laugh, nor to inspire others with her warmth and kindness. I admired and respected her — for her energy and commitment to others, and especially for her devotion to her two boys. This week at Balmoral, we have all been trying to help William and Harry come to terms with the devastating loss that they and the rest of us have suffered. No one who knew Diana*

will ever forget her. Millions of others who never met her, but felt they knew her, will remember her. I share in your determination to cherish her memory.'

It went some way toward repairing the damage done by those days of silence.

There was sadness of a different kind a few months later when the Queen's beloved Royal Yacht Britannia – the location of so many happy times - was decommissioned. As she said goodbye, Her Majesty was visibly in tears.

The turbulent 90s ended on a hopeful note when the Queen's youngest son, Prince Edward, married his long-term girlfriend, Sophie Rees Jones, in June 1999.

Above:
Diana's coffin borne through the streets of London on its way to Westminster Abbey. Her coffin was draped in a pall depicting the royal standard with an ermine border

The Noughties onwards

Losing both her sister and her mother in the space of seven weeks in early 2002, hit Elizabeth hard. But, as always, duty to the crown prevailed. There was much to celebrate during these early years of the new millennium – her 2002 Golden Jubilee, the births of two last grandchildren Louise and James, the 2005 wedding of Prince Charles to Camilla, whom the Queen had come to realise was non-negotiable as far as her son was involved, and then in 2011, the marriage of Prince William to Catherine Middleton and the subsequent arrival of their three children. However, all was not sweetness and light within the family. The issue lay with Elizabeth's so-called 'favourite' son, Andrew.

The BBC in March 2011 reported that Andrew's friendship with Jeffrey Epstein, an American financier and convicted sex offender was producing *'a steady stream of criticism'*, and there were calls for him to step down from his role as trade envoy. The Duke was also criticised in the media after his former wife, Sarah, disclosed that he helped arrange for Epstein to pay off £15,000 of her debts. Andrew had been photographed in December 2010 strolling with Epstein during a visit to New York City. In July 2011, the Duke's role as trade envoy was terminated and he reportedly cut all ties with Epstein. In 2014, it was alleged that Andrew was one of several prominent figures to have participated in sexual activities with a minor later identified as Virginia Giuffre (then known by her maiden name Virginia Roberts), who was allegedly trafficked for sex by Epstein. In January 2015, there was renewed media and public pressure for Buckingham Palace to explain Andrew's connection with Epstein. Buckingham Palace stated that *'any suggestion of impropriety with underage minors is categorically untrue'* and later repeated the denial. Requests from Giuffre's lawyers for a statement from the Duke of York, under oath, about the allegations were returned unanswered. But the furore didn't die down. Following intense negative reaction to his connections to Epstein, Andrew permanently resigned from public roles in May 2020 and his honorary military affiliations and royal charitable patronages were returned to the Queen in January 2022. At the time of writing, Andrew is the defendant in a civil lawsuit over sexual assault, filed by Giuffre in New York State.

At the time of writing it is reported that Andrew has agreed to settle the civil lawsuit for a reputed amount in the millions of pounds.

Below:
The Duke of York spoke about his links to Jeffrey Epstein in an interview with BBC Newsnight's Emily Maitlis

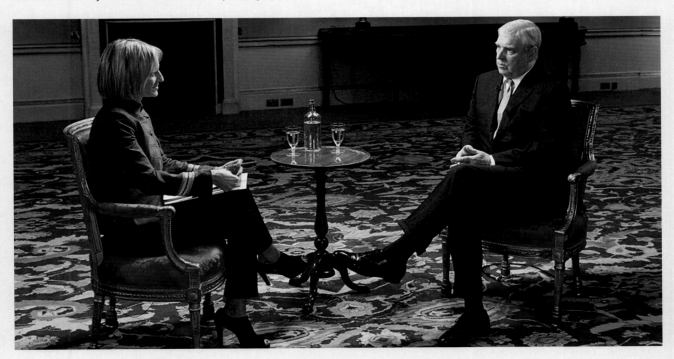

In accordance with the *'never complain, never explain'* mantra by which she has lived her life, the Queen's feelings regarding these allegations towards her son have not been made public. However, it's said that Her Majesty was *'saddened'* at having to force Prince Andrew out of the Royal Family but backed Prince Charles in saying he had *'run out of road'*. The fear is that a potential court case will completely overshadow the Platinum Jubilee Celebrations.

In addition to seeing her late husband becoming increasingly ill over the past few years and mourning his death in April 2021, the Queen has also had to deal with 'Megxit' – ie, her beloved grandson Prince Harry and wife Megan Markle, whom he married in May 2018, turning their back on Royal duties and later sitting down to do a *'warts and all'* interview with Oprah in which, amongst other things, the Royal family were branded as racist.

With the publication of Prince Harry's memoirs due later this year, Her Majesty should perhaps brace herself.

Right:
Queen Elizabeth II arrives for the funeral of Prince Philip, Duke of Edinburgh at St George's Chapel at Windsor Castle on April 17, 2021 in Windsor. Only 30 guests could be invited due to Coronavirus pandemic restrictions

Below:
A selection of British newspaper publications in response to the Meghan, Duchess of Sussex and Prince Harry, Duke of Sussex's interview with Oprah Winfrey on March 08, 2021 in London, England. The interview first aired in the US on Sunday 7th March on CBS and in the UK on Monday 8th March on ITV

Celebrations and Jubilee Jubilations

The Queen, June 2002

'Gratitude, respect and pride, these words sum up how I feel about the people of this country and the Commonwealth – and what this Golden Jubilee means to me'

The Queen's reign has seen an unprecedented series of milestones. Her Majesty's jubilees and landmark birthdays and anniversaries have provided cause for celebration and reflection throughout the remarkable years since her Accession. These events reinforce the monarch's role as a focus for national identity and unity around the United Kingdom and also the Commonwealth.

Below:
The Queen at the unveiling of a Scented Garden for the Blind, Haverstoe Park, Cleethorpes, 1977

The Silver Jubilee

In 1977 Her Majesty's Silver Jubilee was marked with celebrations throughout the UK and Commonwealth. The actual 25th anniversary of the Queen's Accession on 6 February 1952 was commemorated in church services throughout that month. The Queen spent the anniversary weekend at Windsor with her family with full jubilee celebrations beginning in the summer of 1977.

During these months she embarked on a large-scale tour, having decided that she wished to mark her jubilee by meeting as many of her people as possible. No other Sovereign had visited so much of Britain in the course of just three months - the six jubilee tours in the UK and Northern Ireland covered 36 counties. The home tours began in Glasgow on 17 May, with greater crowds than the city had ever seen before. The tours continued throughout England and Wales - in Lancashire over a million people turned out on one day - before culminating in a visit to Northern Ireland. Official overseas visits were also made to Western Samoa, Australia, New Zealand, Tonga, Fiji, Tasmania, Papua New Guinea, Canada and the West Indies. During the year it was estimated that the Queen and the Duke of Edinburgh travelled 56,000 miles.

The climax of the national celebrations came in early June. On the evening of Monday 6 June, the Queen lit a bonfire beacon at Windsor which started a chain of beacons across the country. On Tuesday 7 June, vast crowds lined the London streets to see her drive in the Gold State Coach to St Paul's Cathedral for a Service of Thanksgiving attended by heads of state from around the world and former prime ministers of the UK. Afterwards the Queen and members of the Royal Family attended a lunch at the Guildhall, at which Her Majesty made the following speech.

'My Lord Mayor, when I was 21, I pledged

Above:
Commemorative Teapot marking H.M.Queen Elizabeth II Silver Jubilee in 1977

my life to the service of our people and I asked for God's help to make good that vow. Although that vow was made in my salad days, when I was green in judgement, I do not regret nor retract one word of it.'

An estimated 500 million people watched on television as the procession returned down the Mall. Back at Buckingham Palace, The Queen made several balcony appearances. Street parties and village parties started up all over the country - in London alone 4,000 were reported to have been held. The final event of the central week of celebrations was a river progress down the Thames from Greenwich to Lambeth on Thursday 9 June, emulating the ceremonial barge trips of Elizabeth I. After the Queen had opened the Silver Jubilee Walkway and the new South Bank Jubilee Gardens, the journey ended with a firework display, and a procession of lighted carriages took the Queen back to Buckingham Palace for more balcony appearances to a cheering crowd.

The Golden Jubilee

A packed programme of events took place in 2002 to celebrate 50 years of the Queen's reign. Six key Jubilee themes shaped events - Celebration, Community, Service, Past and future, Giving thanks and Commonwealth. The Queen and the Duke of Edinburgh undertook extensive tours of the Commonwealth and the UK, leading to an extraordinarily busy year for the royal couple. They attended a dinner hosted by Prime Minister Tony Blair at 10 Downing Street and also a session of the joint Houses of the Houses of Parliament in Westminster Hall at which Her Majesty addressed both Houses. They also gave a dinner for representatives of the Armed Services at Windsor Castle and visited the Armed Forces in Portsmouth.

The central focus for the year was the Jubilee weekend in June 2002 which began with a classical music concert in the gardens at Buckingham Palace. There was a Jubilee Church Service at St George's Chapel in Windsor and a National Service of Thanksgiving at St Paul's Cathedral which followed a Ceremonial Procession from Buckingham Palace. Events culminated in a pop concert at Buckingham Palace with performers including Paul McCartney, Bryan Adams, Elton John and Shirley Bassey.

The evening ended with a spectacular, fireworks display and The Queen lighting the National Beacon, the last in a string of 2,006 beacons which had been lit in a chain across the Commonwealth.

During a lunch at Guildhall, London, on 4 June 2002, Her Majesty made a speech in which she thanked the nation for their support throughout her reign.

Above:
Fireworks burst over Buckingham Palace in London Monday 03 June 2002, after Britain's Queen Elizabeth II lit a beacon to commemorate her Golden Jubilee. Earlier, some 12 000 people had watched the Party in the Palace - a crowd estimated at one million gathered outside to enjoy the music

Left:
Queen Elizabeth II greeting well wishers during her visit to Duthie Park, to mark her continuing Golden Jubilee tour

Right:
Arriva London South Routemaster bus RM6 wearing the special gold livery & jubilee logos applied to mark the Golden Jubilee of Elizabeth II

The Queen's 80th birthday

The Queen turned 80 on 21 April 2006, celebrating her official birthday on 17 June 2006. A number of events took place to celebrate both occasions. A unique children's party was held at Buckingham Palace to celebrate the magic of books. Two thousand children were invited, and a stage performance – during which the Queen made a cameo appearance – was broadcast live on TV. Trooping the Colour marked Her Majesty's official birthday as it does every year, but to mark the special occasion, a spectacular flypast and a 'feu de joie' or 'fire of joy' were added to the traditional celebrations.

Services of Thanksgiving were held at St George's Chapel in Windsor and at St Paul's Cathedral. The Queen celebrated with others of her generation who had similarly led a life of service and dedication at a 'Service over 60' reception hosted by Her Majesty, which celebrated guests over the age of 60 who had made a significant contribution to national life, as did the 'Help the Aged Living Legends Awards' at Windsor Castle. On 19 April, guests celebrating their 80th birthdays on the same day as her were invited to Buckingham Palace for a reception. The Queen spent her actual birthday meeting the crowds on a walkabout in Windsor before attending a private family dinner at the newly restored Kew Palace hosted by Prince Charles, followed by a spectacular fireworks display. Her Majesty received almost 40,000 birthday messages from members of the public during her 80th birthday year.

Right:
HM Queen Elizabeth II sits in the Regency Room at Buckingham Palace in London, April 20, 2006, as she looks at some of the cards which have been sent to her for her 80th birthday

Below:
Queen Elizabeth II stands with Prince Philip, Duke of Edinburgh and the rest of her family to watch a firework display at Kew Palace in west London, to celebrate her 80th birthday on April 21, 2006

Diamond Wedding anniversary

The Queen and The Duke of Edinburgh celebrated their 60th wedding anniversary on 20 November 2007. Events to mark the anniversary included a Service of Celebration at Westminster Abbey followed by the unveiling of a new Jubilee Walkway panoramic panel in Parliament Square. The couple also returned to the location of their honeymoon - Broadlands in Hampshire, home of Prince Philip's uncle, Earl Mountbatten, to recreate the photographs which had been taken 60 years previously.

Right

HM The Queen Elizabeth II and Prince Philip, The Duke of Edinburgh re-visit Broadlands, to mark their Diamond Wedding Anniversary on November 20. The royals spent their wedding night at Broadlands in Hampshire in November 1947, the former home of Prince Philip's uncle, Earl Mountbatten

The Diamond Jubilee

The Diamond Jubilee in 2012 was marked with a spectacular central weekend and a series of regional tours throughout the UK and Commonwealth. The central weekend in June began with the Queen's visit to the Epsom Derby on the Saturday. On the Sunday, 'Big Jubilee Lunches' were held across the UK - building on the already popular 'Big Lunch' initiative where people were encouraged to share lunch with neighbours and friends as part of the Diamond Jubilee celebrations. The Thames Diamond Jubilee Pageant also took place on the Sunday, with up to 1,000 boats assembled on the Thames from across the UK, the Commonwealth and around the world. The Queen and The Duke of Edinburgh travelled in the Royal Barge which formed the centrepiece of the flotilla. On the Monday, a host of famous faces came together to celebrate the Diamond Jubilee against the backdrop of Buckingham Palace for a concert organised by Take That singer and songwriter Gary Barlow. Performers included Will.i.am, Stevie Wonder, Grace Jones and Kylie Minogue.

Following the concert, The Queen lit the National Beacon - one of a network of 2,012 which were lit by communities and indi-viduals throughout the UK, Channel Islands, the Isle of Man and the Commonwealth. The Diamond Jubilee weekend culminated with a day of celebrations in central London, including a service at St Paul's Cathedral followed by two receptions, a lunch at Westminster Hall, a Carriage Procession to Buckingham Palace and finally a Balcony appearance, Flypast, and Feu de Joie.

Right:
Following a nationwide competition this emblem from 10-year-old Katherine Dewar was chosen as the winning Diamond Jubilee logo

Far Right:
Prince Philip, Duke of Edinburgh and Queen Elizabeth II wave from the Spirit of Chartwell during the Diamond Jubilee Thames River Pageant on June 3, 2012 in London

Below:
Queen Elizabeth II meets performers (L-R) Sir Cliff Richard, Dame Shirley Bassey, Sir Tom Jones and Sir Paul McCartney backstage after the Diamond Jubilee, Buckingham Palace Concert on June 04, 2012

Longest Reigning Monarch

On 9 September 2015 the Queen became Britain's Longest Reigning Monarch, surpassing the 63 year and 216 day reign of her great, great grandmother Queen Victoria. Although a landmark date, the day was treated like any other as the Queen and Prince Philip travelled by steam train from Edinburgh to Tweedbank, where she formally opened the new Scottish Borders Railway. However, she did refer to the milestone in her speech.

Below:
The Queen delivering a speech at the official opening of the Borders Railway, on the day she became the longest reigning British monarch

'Many have kindly noted another significance attaching to today, although it is not one to which I have ever aspired,' she said. 'Inevitably, a long life can pass by many milestones – my own is no exception. But I thank you all, and the many others at home and overseas, for your touching messages of great kindness.'

The Queen's 90th birthday

The Queen celebrated her 90th birthday on 21 April 2016 and her official birthday on 11 June 2016, the second day of three days of national celebrations. Her Majesty's actual birthday was spent in Windsor where she met well-wishers during a walkabout in the town centre and met others celebrating their 90th birthdays, before unveiling a plaque marking The Queen's Walkway. Later in the evening, Her Majesty, with the Prince of Wales, lit the principal beacon which set in train a series of over 900 beacons across the country and worldwide to celebrate her momentous milestone. On June 10 2016, the Queen and the Duke of Edinburgh were joined by members of the Royal Family of a National Service of Thanksgiving at St Paul's Cathedral. On June 11 2016, the Queen's official birthday, Her Majesty was joined by members of her family at The Queen's Birthday Parade on Horse Guards Parade, followed by an appearance on the balcony of Buckingham Palace with a Flypast. On June 12 2016 a huge street party and parade took place on the Mall - The Patron's Lunch - a celebration of over 600 charities and organisations that the Queen was Patron of. In a speech, the Duke of Cambridge paid tribute to his Granny.

'My family has had plenty of reason to celebrate since the Queen turned 90 in April. The Queen's strong health and relentless energy, her sharp wit and famous sense of humour, and the fact that the Queen remains very much at the helm of our family, our nation and the Commonwealth. Granny, thank you for everything you have done for your family. We could not wish you a happier birthday.'

Above:
31 Aircraft mark The Queen's 90th Birthday with a flypast

The Sapphire Jubilee

February 6 2017 marked 65 years since the Queen acceded to the throne, becoming the first British Monarch to mark their Sapphire Jubilee. To coincide with the occasion Buckingham Palace re-released a photograph of Her Majesty taken by David Bailey in 2014. In the photograph, the Queen is wearing a suite of sapphire jewellery given to her by King George VI as a wedding gift in 1947.

Below:
Prince William, Duke of Cambridge admires the David Bailey Portrait of the Queen

The Platinum Jubilee

In 2022, Her Majesty becomes the first British Monarch to celebrate a Platinum Jubilee, marking 70 years of service to the people of the United Kingdom and the Commonwealth. To celebrate this unprecedented anniversary, events and initiatives are taking place throughout the year, culminating in a four-day UK bank holiday weekend from Thursday 2 to Sunday 5 June. The four days of celebrations include public events and community activities, as well as national moments of reflection on The Queen's 70 years of service. These include The Trooping of the Colour on June 2 when over 1,400 parading soldiers, 200 horses and 400 musicians will come together in the traditional Parade to mark the Queen's official birthday, usually held on the second Saturday in June. The Parade closes with the traditional RAF fly-past, watched by The Queen and Members of the Royal Family from the Buckingham Palace balcony.

The UK's long tradition of celebrating Royal Jubilees, Weddings and Coronations with the lighting of beacons will be continued to mark the Platinum Jubilee. Over 1,500 beacons will be lit throughout the United Kingdom, Channel Islands, Isle of Man and UK overseas territories. For the first time, beacons will also be lit in each of the capital cities of the Commonwealth countries to celebrate The Queen's Platinum Jubilee. The main beacon will be lit in a special ceremony at Buckingham Palace. On Friday 3 June, a Service of Thanksgiving for the Queen's reign will be held at St Paul's Cathedral. On Saturday 4 June, Her Majesty accompanied by Members of the Royal Family, will attend the Derby at Epsom Downs. That evening the BBC will stage and broadcast a special live concert from Buckingham Palace that will bring together some of the world's biggest entertainment stars to celebrate the most significant and joyous moments from The Queen's seven-decade reign. On Sunday June 5, The Big Jubilee Lunch will take place, encouraging communities to celebrate their connections and get to know each other a little bit better, coming together in a spirit of fun and friendship. Later on, The Platinum Jubilee Pageant takes place in London at which artistic performers, dancers, musicians, military personnel, key workers and volunteers will unite to tell the story of The Queen's 70-year reign in an awe-inspiring festival of creativity. Forming an important part of the pageant the 'River of Hope' section will comprise of two hundred silk flags which will process down The Mall, appearing like a moving river.

Below:

Images of Britain's Queen Elizabeth II are displayed on the big digital screens at Piccadilly Circus in central London on February 6, 2022, to mark the start of Her Majesty's Platinum Jubilee Year

Britain's Queen Elizabeth II looking at Queen Victoria's Autograph
fan, alongside a display of memorabilia from her Golden and Platinum
Jubilees, in the Oak Room at Windsor Castle, west of London

Off Duty

Queen Elizabeth II

'I should like to be a horse'

The Queen may be the longest reigning monarch in British history and will surely go down in the annals of time as the most successful of sovereigns but it's widely thought that given the choice, she would have preferred to be a 'lady living in the country with lots of horses and dogs,' as she once confided to a lady in waiting. Horses and dogs are an absolute passion – possibly because her animals neither know nor care that she is Queen. Her love for her dogs and horses humanizes her. While she may be a monarch, she is also a woman who just loves her pets.

Right:
Queen Elizabeth II seen horse riding in the grounds of Windsor Castle on March 30, 2007

Far Right:
Queen Elizabeth II of England at Balmoral Castle with one of her Corgis, 28th September 1952

It's a Dog's Life

While King George VI brought home the first corgi, Dookie, when Queen Elizabeth was just a child, she didn't receive her own personal dog until she was 18. As a birthday present, the future queen was gifted with Susan, a female corgi who remained with her for 14 years. The story goes that the then Princess Elizabeth snuck Susan into her carriage on her wedding day in 1947. She also insisted on having her beloved pet accompany her as she and husband Prince Philip honeymooned at Scotland's Balmoral Castle. Susan died in January 1959 but she left a legacy by instigating Elizabeth's interest in breeding. For many years to come, there were corgis who hailed from Susan's lineage - the last of Susan's descendants, Willow, died in 2018. It was Queen Elizabeth who actually invented 'the dorgi' - a combination of corgi and dachshund. The genesis of the breed happened quite by accident. The Queen's sister, Princess Margaret, had a dachshund named Pipkin who had an unplanned opportunity to get close to one of the queen's corgis, named Tiny, and, nature having taken its course, along came a litter of puppies. The serendipitous breeding was such a hit that the family kept up the tradition with several dorgis following. The end of the line stopped with Vulcan who died in 2020. The appearance of the Queen with her pack of corgis and dorgis was such a vision that even Princess Diana commented on it.

'The Queen is always surrounded by corgis so you get the feeling you are standing on a moving carpet,' she once said.

When Her Majesty was briefly hospitalized in October 2021, she was later given strict instructions by her doctors to rest — and this included no dog walks for a week. It was reportedly a huge blow to Elizabeth, who considers the activity her *'tonic'*. Thankfully, she was limited from her daily delight only for a week.

Her corgis and dorgis are hugely important to her,' says Royal biographer Penelope Junor *'They have over the years been closer to her than any human being. They are intensely loyal and have never let her down.'*

Queen Elizabeth even makes Christmas stockings for her dogs, stuffing them with treats and presents. They clearly are pampered pooches. There is said to be a special room for the dogs in each of Her Majesty's homes where they sleep in wicker baskets lined with bedding that is changed daily and the pets are watched over by footmen. The canines also dine on doggy haute cuisine!

'The dogs would have a whole selection of different meats, cabbage, and rice,' says former royal chef, Darren McGrady. *'The meat had to be cut into a fine dice to be sure that there were no bones.'*

Queen Elizabeth apparently is in charge of food distribution

herself - feeding them in order of pack hierarchy by arranging them in a circle and dolling out the carefully prepared dishes.

In 2018, it was noted that the royal corgi/dorgi population was dwindling. Queen Elizabeth had previously expressed her desire to stop breeding dogs so as not to *'leave any young dog behind'*.

___

Above Left:
Princess Elizabeth, now Queen Elizabeth II with two corgi dogs at her home at 145 Piccadilly, London, July 1936

Above Right:
Queen Elizabeth II at Sandringham with Her Corgies, 1980

Right:
Queen Elizabeth II arrives at Aberdeen Airport with her corgis to start her holidays in Balmoral, Scotland in 1974

She was also said to be concerned about the potential *'tripping hazard'* of energetic dogs getting underfoot. Her main fear is that if she fell and broke her arm or even a leg, she would not be able to perform her duties for many weeks if not months. But two months ahead of her 95th birthday in April 2021, the Queen took possession of two pups - a corgi named Muick and a dorgi called Fergus, the latter of whom sadly died in May 2021. Notably, they were the first to not come from her first dog, Susan's, lineage. But they were said to have been a great comfort to Her Majesty during Prince Philip's final illness and subsequent passing. At the royal residence Sandringham House, there is a pet graveyard that has been in use since 1887 when Queen Victoria buried a collie named Noble.

Since then, Queen Elizabeth has used the designated area as the location for burying her dogs, with *'commissioned gravestones'* honouring her beloved pets.

In addition to the Royal corgi/dorgi community, the Queen has a deep fondness for her Labradors – there are reported to be up to 20 of them – who are based at Sandringham. It's believed that the fleet of Land Rovers at her Norfolk home are custom-made with windscreen wipers on the inside, specifically because the labradors have a tendency to steam cars up from the inside out!

A Horse, a Horse... My 'Queendom' for a Horse!

While the Queen's horses may not be pets in the traditional sense, she obviously loves her equine companions and there has always been a close bond between royal rider and horse. Her first riding lesson took place when she was just three years old and she has continued to ride throughout her life. Even at age 94 in 2020, the queen was spotted near Windsor Castle taking a turn around the grounds on her fell pony. However, her interest extends far beyond simply going out for a ride or hack. Horse racing is a passion and she is an expert, having bred winners since the early days of her reign.

'It's an in-built passion,' says John Warren, Bloodstock & Racing Advisor to Her Majesty. *'It started when she was a teenager and she had hairy little ponies - then her father introduced her to a thoroughbred. When she touched the skin of the thorough-bred she didn't want to wash her hands for the rest of the day, so she got really addicted to it very young and nothing has diminished or changed over all these years.'*

When Elizabeth became monarch in 1952, she inherited the royal colours - purple, gold braid, scarlet sleeves, black velvet cap with gold fringe. These colours have gone on to see great success in the last 70 years whilst she has owned them. Her first winner came just months after she inherited the colours when 'Choir Boy' passed the winning post to claim the Wilburton Handicap at Newmarket in May 1952. The Queen currently has won over 1,600 races making her one of the most successful racehorse owners in history. She has also won every one of the five British Classic Races, multiple times, except the Epsom Derby, a race that the Queen has yet to grasp finishing agonizingly close in the year of her coronation, 1953, where 'Aureole' finished second to 'Pinza'. It is hoped that Her Majesty will finally achieve this in her Platinum Jubilee year with 'Reach for The Moon'. In 1954 and 1957, she was named British flat racing Champion Owner, the first reigning monarch ever to do so twice.

Above:

The Queen and President Reagan riding at Windsor, June 1982

Left:

Princess Elizabeth out riding at the Royal Lodge, Windsor, April 1940

She also won the Racehorse Owners Association Owner of the Year award in 2013 after her magnificent win with 'Estimate' in the Ascot Gold Cup. There are three races named in honour of the Queen, those being the Queen Elizabeth II Challenge Cup Stakes, the Queen Elizabeth II Commemorative Cup and the Queen Elizabeth II Stakes.

'I think this is her passion in life, and she loves it and you can tell how much she loves it,' her daughter-in-law, the Duchess of Cornwall, has remarked. *'She can tell you every horse she's bred and owned, from the very beginning, she doesn't forget anything. She's encyclopeadic about her knowledge.'*

Much like her dogs, Elizabeth's horses seemingly offer a wild, spirited escape from the protocols of royal life.

Below:

Queen Elizabeth II and Frankie Dettori (R) during Royal Ascot 2021 at Ascot Racecourse on June 19, 2021

Right:

Queen Elizabeth II, accompanied by a groom, seen horse riding in the grounds of Windsor Castle on June 10, 2006

At Home

The Queen's home life has always been surprisingly low-profile, revolving around her family and her faith. She may be a monarch but she is also a mother, grandmother, great-grandmother - and friend to a very select group. The Queen has sadly lost a number of close friends over recent years. Her best friend is thought to be Princess Alexandra. They are first cousins and the princess was even one of The Queen's bridesmaids in 1947. It is with loved ones that Elizabeth can truly be herself – a kind, thoughtful woman with a gift for mimicry and a great sense of humour who also possesses the kind of wisdom that comes with having lived a long life.

In the past Her Majesty loved nothing more than an impromptu trip to the theatre when she and Prince Philip would make incognito trips to the West End to see plays such as 'War horse' and musicals like 'Billy Elliot'.

'The Queen loves the theatre and musicals like "Showboat", "Oklahoma!" and "Annie Get Your Gun",' royal party planner, the late Lady Elizabeth Anson, revealed in 2011.'These were the tunes that remained in one's head and were very danceable to. The Queen is also a fantastic dancer. She's got great rhythm.'

Her Majesty is said to love ABBA – especially 'Dancing Queen' – and has a soft spot in her heart for Scottish Country dancing. Every year while at Balmoral, the queen hosts a dance for neighbours, estate and castle staff and people from the local community. Other 'off-duty' interests include walking – especially when at Balmoral where she also enjoys hosting intimate barbeques and doing the washing-up herself, gardening and stamp collecting! Dinner at a restaurant or hotel has also been regarded as a rare treat – The Goring near Buckingham Palace, where the Middleton family spent the night before Kate and Wills' wedding, is a particular favourite.

Above:

28th September 1952: Princess Elizabeth watching her son
Prince Charles playing in his toy car while at Balmoral

Left:

Queen Elizabeth II and Prince Philip, the Duke of Edinburgh
(1921 - 2021) with their sons Prince Andrew (left) and Prince
Edward at Balmoral Castle in Scotland, on their Silver Wedding
anniversary year, September 1972

A Day in the Life

A former page to Her Majesty

'Hers is very much a working desk – it may appear cluttered and untidy to the average eye, but the Queen knows where everything is and hates it if anything is moved without her permission'

Pre-pandemic, the Queen's routine followed a well-trodden, time-honoured path regardless of what home she happened to be staying in. December to early February would see her based at Sandringham in Norfolk, three weekdays from February onwards she would be resident at Buckingham Palace in London while long weekends were spent at nearby Windsor Castle. July would see her heading to Balmoral in the Scottish Islands where she stayed until October before heading back to London and Windsor. The lockdowns were spent at Windsor – widely thought to be her favourite residence as she spent much of her childhood there. However, since Prince Philip's passing in April 2021 coupled with Her Majesty cutting back on duties on the advice of doctors, the Queen now spends most of her time at Windsor. However, her daily routine remains much the same.

The Queen wakes each morning at about 7:30 am when her personal maid, having lightly knocked on the door, enters HM's private apartments carrying the 'morning tray' for her royal mistress. The tray contains pots of Earl Grey tea and hot water, both in solid silver, and a jug of cold milk but no sugar. The cup and saucer are bone china and there is also a fine linen napkin draped across the tray embossed with the royal cypher 'E II R'. The maid walks across to the bedside table with its family photographs and telephone and switches on the Roberts radio which is tuned to BBC Radio Four - the Queen likes to wake up to the 'Today' programme in order to keep abreast of the day's news and hear political debates. While Her Majesty is enjoying her first cup of tea in bed – which has sheets, blankets

Right:

Queen Elizabeth II at the writing desk in her study in Balmoral Castle, Scotland, 1972

and an eiderdown rather than a duvet or quilt - her maid goes into the adjoining bathroom to draw the bath, which has to be exactly the right temperature. This is tested with a wooden-cased thermometer and measure no more than seven inches of water. While the Queen is bathing, one of her three dressers, under the supervision of Angela Kelly, the Queen's Personal Assistant and Curator of her Wardrobe, lays out the first outfit of the day in the adjacent dressing room with its floor-to-ceiling mirrors and walk-in wardrobes. Mrs Kelly knows exactly what is needed, as she is given the Queen's daily programme the evening before. The Queen rarely makes her own sartorial choices. That, she says, is why she employs dressers. Once bathed and dressed, her hairdresser arrives to arrange her hair in the bouffant style she's had for many years.

Breakfast is served promptly at 8.30 in the Queen's own private dining room. The meal tends to be continentally themed, comprising of cereal, yoghurt and toast, although Her Majesty is said to request kippers occasionally. As she eats, a lone piper from one of the Scottish regiments marches up and down on the terrace below – a longstanding royal tradition dating back to Queen Victoria's time. By 9.30, the Queen will be at her desk in her comfortably furnished-rather-than-luxurious office, and be working through paperwork. A heavy crystal double inkwell on her desk contains the black ink the Queen uses to sign official documents and the

Above:
Framed photographs of the Royal Family

Right:
Queen Elizabeth II and Prince Philip sort through a basket of mail on the occasion of their 25th wedding anniversary, 1972

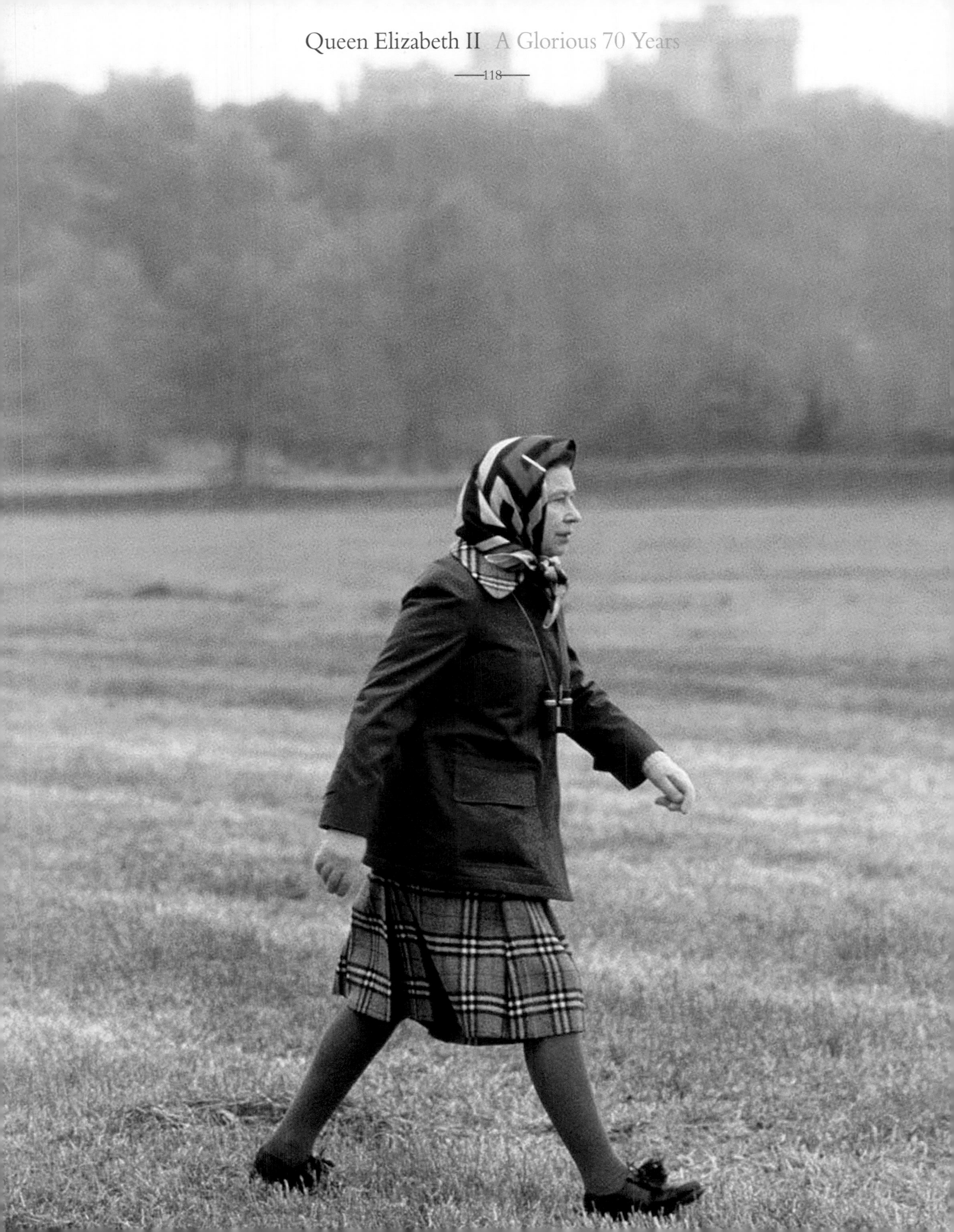

special green colour she likes for personal letters. She rarely uses a ballpoint pen, insisting on her favourite old fountain pen. A pristine sheet of blotting paper is replaced every day. It is coloured black so that no trace of Her Majesty's writing can be seen.

Her press secretary will have prepared a digest of the day's news from the morning radio and television. Once the Queen has read this anthology and other relevant documents, her private secretary arrives with the papers she is required to read through and initial. The Queen is addressed initially as '*Your Majesty*', accompanied by a brief bow from the neck, and then as '*Ma'am*' to rhyme with '*jam*' rather than '*Marm*' with '*harm*'. The Queen's mailbox normally runs to scores of items every day, so she has mastered the knack of 'scanning' or speed-reading.

'*It is fortunate,*' she has commented, '*that I am quite a quick reader.*'

If guests are expected at the Castle, the housekeeper is summoned so that domestic arrangements for their comfort can be discussed. Later in the morning, the duty lady-in-waiting is called to attend on the Queen. Her Majesty may show her attendant some of the letters she has received which require a personal reply.

'*I always feel that letters are rather personal to oneself,*' she has said. '*People write them thinking that I'm going to read them. I don't open and read them all because I don't have time to do that. Letters certainly give me an idea of what is worrying people and what they feel I could do to help. There are occasions when I can help and pass things on to the right authorities. Or even in some cases, write to various organisations who will look into the issue at hand. Letters are written to me and I want to see what people are saying. One often feels that the buck stops here.*'

Those from children and the elderly get extra special attention with the lady-in-waiting relying and signing the letters on the

Left:

The Queen in laced up brogue shoes and raincoat walking in Windsor Great Park in the grounds of Windsor Castle in 1985

Queen's behalf. Personal friends who correspond with her write their initials in the lower left-hand corner of the envelope and, when the staff see these, they know not to open them as the Queen likes to open her private post personally.

Official guests have an audience – either virtual or in person - at around midday. If in the latter category, these take place in the Audience Room, also part of the Queen's suite, and last for around ten minutes.

Lunch is usually eaten alone. Her Majesty prefers light meals, but although the dishes may be simple they are always beautifully presented — every vegetable matching each other in shape and size. A typical lunch, served at 1pm, would be fish and vegetables, such as a grilled Dover sole on a bed of wilted spinach or courgettes. It is said Her Majesty avoids carbohydrates. She drinks her favourite still Malvern water – a brand of natural spring water sourced from the Malvern Hills near Wales. The royal chef will have previously sent a list to Her Majesty, containing three suggestions for every meal during the coming week. It is returned when she has indicated what she wants. All menus continue to be written in French, this having been the official language at Court since Queen Victoria's reign, when her French head chef insisted on French cuisine and handwritten menus in French.

Immediately after lunch, the Queen likes to walk in the gardens with her dogs. Household staff know to keep out of the way at this time as she doesn't welcome company or want to see anyone else in the gardens. Occasionally she may be accompanied by a family member if they have joined her for lunch. Then she relaxes for half an hour with the Racing Post – the 'go to' publication of the horse racing community. The afternoon may well be taken up with engagements, although many of these are virtual since

Right:

Queen Elizabeth II and Prince Philip relax at Balmoral castle in this photo, the year 1977 marks the 25th year of her reign as the British sovereign and the 30th anniversary of her wedding

the pandemic. All afternoon meetings are scheduled to finish before 4.30 so that the Queen can be free for afternoon tea in her personal sitting room.

'Her sitting room is comfortable and a bit old-fashioned with chintz-type furnishings,' says a former Royal Protection Officer to Her Majesty. *'It is the kind of sitting room many well-to-do grandmothers may have.'*

Any family visits will have been booked in advance – there is no *'dropping by'* because mummy, granny or auntie is The Queen! Royal grandchildren who attended school at Eton – eg, Princes William and Harry - have remarked they visited Her Majesty at Windsor quite often during their school days as it is just across the river from the castle. Her daughter-in-law, Sophie Countess of Wessex, is said to be a favourite afternoon tea companion as are Her Majesty's ladies in waiting. The kitchens send up Earl Grey tea and a few varieties of finger sandwiches. These include smoked salmon, cucumber, ham and mustard or egg mayonnaise. There are always jam pennies – Her Majesty's favourites – which are jam sandwiches cut into rounds the size of an old penny. Tiny scones with jam and cream, Dundee fruit cake and Chocolate biscuit cake, made with Rich Tea biscuits, often accompany the sweets and sandwiches. The ritual never changes and neither does the fare. After tea, Her Majesty returns to her office for another hour. If there is no evening engagement, the Queen retires to her own rooms to rest before dinner at 8pm. This for the Queen is the most relaxed meal of the day, sometimes

eaten off a silver tray. Dinner is almost always sourced from the royal stocks, including game or fish from Sandringham, or venison or salmon from Balmoral, but with no potatoes, rice or pasta. For dessert, Her Majesty is fond of Windsor-grown white peaches. She used to enjoy a martini or gin and dubonnet before dinner and a glass of wine with her meal but on the advice of her doctors, she no longer drinks alcohol. The Queen likes to remain in her private quarters, reading or watching television in her sitting room while she eats. Her Majesty enjoys watching TV – her favourite shows are said to include costume dramas like 'Downton Abbey', murder mysteries such as 'Midsomer Murders', the likes of 'Coronation Street and Eastenders', and old-school sitcoms like 'Dad's Army'. She frequently spends part of the evening working on her red boxes. Every evening, a report on the day's proceedings in Parliament is delivered to her, written by the Vice-Chamberlain of the Household, who is a senior MP, and this she reads before she retires.

Her Majesty is not a night owl - she is usually in bed by 11pm but likes to read for a while. Her favourite relaxation is to read the latest Dick Francis racing novel and she is sent the first copy of every first edition, always in hard back. The tradition continues now Dick's son Felix has taken over writing the bestsellers.

Routine rules in the Royal household and the next day, Her Majesty will do it all over again.

Left:

The Queen's role as head of state means that she needs to keep abreast of what is happening in Parliament and the governments of all the other Commonwealth countries, as well as current events from around the world. Documents to which the monarch must give her signature and royal assent are delivered to her in red despatch boxes, which the Queen addresses daily

Right:

Queen Elizabeth II studies one of the first copies of 'Queen Elizabeth the Queen Mother, The Official Biography' in a living room at Birkhall the Scottish home of the Prince of Wales and Duchess of Cornwall on September 2, 2009

Style Icon

Her Majesty, Queen Elizabeth II

'If I wore beige, nobody would know who I am'

I n the 70 years she has been on the throne, Queen Elizabeth II has worn every colour of the rainbow. . . and then some – yellows, purples, blues, pinks, reds, green, silver, gold, orange, black, white, browns and combinations of all of them. On occasion florescent shades, too.

'She needs to stand out for people to be able to say "I saw the queen,"' her daughter-in-law, Sophie, Countess of Wessex, said in the TV documentary 'The Queen at 90'. *'Don't forget that when she turns up somewhere, the crowds are two, three, four, 10, 15 deep, and someone wants to be able to say they saw a bit of the queen's hat as she went past.'*

Although naturally conservative with a small 'c', the Queen is considered a fashion icon who has stood the test of time. Resilient, classic and bold, the monarch has become a trendsetter in her own right. She demonstrates her status by staying exactly the same. Instead of relying on the attention-grabbing power of constant transformation, her image works on a deeper level. By never changing, she blurs the distinction between real woman and royal image.

Left:

Her Majesty the Queen wearing pink during her visit to HMS Ocean in Devonport at a ceremony to rededicate the ship

Right:

Queen Elizabeth II attends the Sunday service at the church of St Mary the Virgin in Flitcham in a striking purple outfit on January 15, 2017 near King's Lynn

her colourful, clean-cut coats, architectural hats, pearls and jersey gloves and those much-loved sturdy shoes and bags. She has, over the decades, given a nod to the style-du-jour – for instance Dior's 'New Look' of the late 1940s and early 1950s, above-the-knee dresses in the 1960s, turban headwear in the '70s, shoulder pads in the 1980s and so on - but she has never allowed herself to be greatly influenced by fickle, everchanging fashion trends.

Hers is a working wardrobe and the demands upon it are truly unique. She must look timeless yet also regal. She must be easy to spot in a vast crowd yet feel comfortable enough to wear outfits for long periods of time and in differing weather conditions. Her clothes must be crease-proof, her hems stable and her headwear wind-proof. That's a given.

A mistress of diplomacy, Her Majesty has always used clothes to flatter and impress her hosts when overseas. In 1960, for example, Thailand's king presented the Queen with the country's highest order of chivalry. When the Queen attended a state dinner in Bangkok in 1972, she wore a Hartnell dress designed specifically to match the yellow sash and insignia she was gifted twelve years earlier — a gesture that was as eloquent as any speech. In 1986, she became the first British monarch to visit China, and dined with leader Deng Xiaoping in a dress adorned with China's national flower. With the Reagans in 1983, she wore a colourful compliment in the form of California poppies, almost as important as her verbal thanks to the U.S. for helping in the Falkland Islands war a year earlier. And who can forget the dazzling green outfit that Her Majesty wore to touch down in Dublin on her landmark visit to Ireland in 2011.

As children, Princess Elizabeth and her younger sister Margaret often wore matching outfits such as traditional smock dresses, classic tweed coats with velvet collars, knee-high socks and Mary Jane shoes. The Duchess of Cambridge dresses her daughter Princess Charlotte in a similarly classic style for formal occasions. As a teenager, Elizabeth's increasingly grown-up wardrobe included suits and dresses tailored by royal couturier Madame Handley-Seymour, as well as wartime hand-me-downs including the Hartnell gown the 19-year-old heir apparent wore for a Cecil Beaton photograph in 1945. Hartnell was a favourite of the Princess' and it was he whom she chose to design both her wedding dress and coronation gown.

Over the next 70 years, Her Majesty has made very few fashion faux-pas. Neither overtly ostentations or over-the-top glamorous, she is – and has always been – immediately recognisable with

Above Left:
Britain's Queen Elizabeth, center, poses with her two daughters, Princess Elizabeth, left, and Princess Margaret, in June 1936 in the garden of the Royal Lodge at Windsor

Right:
Queen Elizabeth II laughs during the Royal Windsor Horse Show on May 01, 1976 in Windsor

129

Below:

A conservator attends to outfits
from the Queen's wardrobe during
the press preview of 'Fashioning A
Reign: 90 years Of Style From The
Queen's Wardrobe' at Buckingham
Palace on July 4, 2016

As a young monarch, Elizabeth's wardrobe was dominated by hourglass-shaped gowns for official evening engagements – a perfect example being the New Look-inspired ivory duchesse satin and black velvet dress that Hartnell made for the young Queen in 1952. Also the blue silk and lace dress with matching jacket he created for her to wear at Princess Margaret's 1960 wedding. For the day-time, pretty dresses worn with white Rayne sandals and neat little hats featured heavily. Another favourite designer, Hardy Amies, would introduce vibrant colours and clean shapes to the Queen's daywear throughout that decade. Bold reds, sunshine yellows, lime green, vibrant oranges and turquoise. . . it seems every shade on the colour spectrum suits her colouring. Beige is the only colour she never wears as it is considered too neutral. When Her Majesty tires of an outfit, she is thought to pass it on to one of her dressers. They can either keep to wear or sell on – although a condition is that every label is cut out and any reference to Royalty disposed of.

Although she rarely wears an outfit twice on formal occasions, Her Majesty has always been considered thrifty. While rationing was still in force during the late 40s and early 50s, for instance, her mother's clothes would be reworked into new outfits for her. For 2012's Diamond Jubilee concert at Buckingham Palace, the Queen's appliquéd gold dress was made from fabric that had been in her possession for over 50 years. A glittering silver gown worn in Slovenia four years earlier was made from material she'd had for 20 years. After 70 years on the throne, Her Majesty's working wardrobe is as impressive as it has ever been. Her favourite go-to designers in recent time being her right-hand-woman, Liverpudlian docker's daughter Angela Kelly and also Berkshire-born couturier, Stuart Parvin.

'Working for the Queen is an amazing honour, I have been doing it for nearly twenty years now and it's an incredible honour,' he has commented. *'It's still exciting to see her arriving in something you've made, always looking so amazing and so radiant. Block colours elongate her – she's only very tiny. She wears so many bright colours, quite outrageous designs and so many prints so fantastically - it's a real privilege! I think possibly my most famous and most memorable dress is a wonderful state gown made out of ivory satin, which was a vintage piece of fabric made specifically for the Queen. She wore it at several state dinners in Parliament but most famously worn for the Annie Leibovitz photographs for the cover of Vanity Fair magazine in 2016. Her Majesty is pictured in the robes and the diadem, it's just an incredible dress.'*

The Queen appears born to wear glamorous gowns and sparkling diadems but it is actually her off-duty, country-casual look she suits the best – so much so that she's been a real influence on generations of fashionistas. Her off-duty wardrobe is as familiar and unchanging as her formalwear. From quilted jackets and weatherproof macs to tweed skirts, kilts and cosy knits, this quintessentially British country style has influenced designers from Dolce & Gabbana to Vivienne Westwood. She is rarely seen without a colourful silk scarf (also worn instead of a riding hat) neatly knotted under the chin while uber-sturdy, brown loafers or lace-ups or wellington boots are a 'shoe-in' for country walks and family picnics.

Her Majesty's favourite 'on-duty' brand footwear has quite a history. In 1950 when Eddie Rayne, the Royal family's shoemaker of choice, was on a trip to New York, a journalist plied him with martinis and managed to find out the Queen's diminutive shoe size. Despite this blip, Rayne shoes remained a key part of the Royal wardrobe for five decades. From 1899, the firm made elegant shoes for theatrical productions and later for Hollywood stars such as Liz Taylor and Ava Gardner. During the early years of her reign, the Queen favoured voguish peep-toe platforms in white suede or leather for day and in colours for evening (in the early 1950s, she was ordering 20-30 pairs a year), but it's the no-nonsense court shoe in calf leather or black patent that would become iconic. With a practical heel of 2 1⁄4 inches and an insole for added comfort, the Royal shoes are 'walked in' by Palace staff – usually Angela Kelly.

'The Queen has very little time to herself and not time to wear in her own shoes,' she has said. 'As we share the same shoe size it makes the most sense this way.'

In 2003, Rayne ceased trading – although they recently relaunched - with the Palace securing the Queen's last pairs from the liquidators. They also tracked down one of the Royal shoemakers, David Hyatt, who had moved to Anello & Davide where the Queen's favourite shoes are still made today.

Just as legendary as her choice of footwear are Her Majesty's bespoke and classically chic 'Launer' handbags. Her Majesty has carried the West Midlands-made design since the 1960s and although she has favoured black patent in the past, she has more recently branched out with different sizes and finishes. Her bags are supplied with a slightly longer handle (more practical when hand-shaking) and are designed to be as lightweight as possible. What's inside the Royal Launer? Mints, a Clarins lipstick, sweeteners, a pair of glasses and lucky charms seems to be the consensus. Her Majesty also puts her handbag to good use when it comes to secretly communicating with her staff. She places it on the floor if she wants to remain conversing with a dignitary. If it's put on a raised surface such as a table or switched from one arm to the other it means that she needs to be immediately 'rescued' from the situation!

As far as make-up goes, Her Majesty is extremely low-maintenance.

'You might be surprised to know that the recording of Her Majesty's Christmas Day broadcast is the only occasion throughout the year when she does not do her own makeup,' says Angela Kelly. 'That's when I arrange for the makeup artist, Marilyn Widdess, to be there on the day of filming.'

Ceremonial Crown Jewels aside, the Queen owns more than 300 items of jewellery, including 98 brooches, 46 necklaces, 37 bracelets, 34 pairs of earrings, 15 rings, 14 watches and 5 pendants. Perhaps the most recognisable of all the Queen's jewellery, though, is the ornate State Diadem which has 1,333 diamonds as well as pearls, silver and gold and was made in 1820 for the coronation of George IV. It was a favourite of Queen Victoria, and was used for Elizabeth's coronation. She has worn it for every state opening of Parliament since 1952.

Left:
Queen Elizabeth II visit to the Mediterranean island of Malta, 1951

Right:
Queen Elizabeth II with a Launer bag in 2015

The elegant Queen Mary's Fringe tiara was originally a necklace given to Queen Mary as a wedding gift by Queen Victoria in 1893. The stones were then used to create a tiara by Garrard in 1919. It was worn by both the Queen and Princess Anne for their wedding days.

The Grand Duchess Vladimir tiara was smuggled out of Russia during the Revolution. It was inherited by the Grand Duchess' daughter, Princess Nicholas of Greece, and then later sold to Queen Mary and inherited by Elizabeth. The Queen last wore this tiara with stunning cabochon emeralds - in place of the pearls - for an Irish state banquet at Windsor in 2014.

Another favourite, the elegant, Russian-style Queen Alexandra Kokoshnik tiara has 488 brilliants and can also be worn as a necklace. It was originally a gift to Queen Alexandra, consort of Edward VII, to mark her silver wedding anniversary, and was later passed down to Queen Mary. It was bequeathed to Elizabeth in 1953.

Also in Her Majesty's collection of tiaras is the Cartier Halo tiara which Kate Middleton wore at her marriage to Prince William in April 2011. Originally purchased by King George VI when Duke of York for his wife-to-be, Elizabeth Bowes Lyon, the tiara has quite a storied history within the royal family, and is of particular significance because it was also gifted to someone who was a non-royal at the time. Given that the Duchess of Cambridge

Above:

Hats belonging to Queen Elizabeth II on display at the exhibition "Hats And Handbags - Accessories From The Royal Wardrobe" at Kensington Palace state apartments. Blue Hat in centre by Milliner Frederick Fox for the Golden Jubilee Day, The lilac/pink hat also by Fox; the green turban, lime green and grey/pink hats by Ian Thomas, and gold looped beret by Simone Mirman

Left:

Queen Elizabeth II in 1959 wearing the Vladimir tiara and the Queen Victoria Jubilee Necklace

design so as not wear out the original piece. So why is the three-strand pearl necklace such a popular item for the monarch?

'It's the necklace that she feels is appropriate,' says Leslie Field, author of 'The Queen's Jewels'. *'She wants to wear pearls every day as her mother and grandmother did before her. She wouldn't wear a diamond necklace to go to a charity lunch — it is simply traditional that a lady would wear pearls during the day.'*

The jewels gifted to the Queen by her beloved husband Philip naturally have great emotional importance. These include a diamond brooch in the shape of his Naval badge, made by Garrard. Philip maintained his career in the Navy until Elizabeth became Queen in 1952, and in those early years, she proudly wore the brooch as a Navy wife. The Queen's engagement ring is diamond and platinum circlet, designed by Prince Philip. It is a classic solitaire set in platinum that features a three-carat diamond, and a collection of accent stones placed on the shoulders. It is made up of diamonds that were initially set in an antique tiara owned by Prince Philip's mother, Princess Alice of Battenburg. Philip used the remaining diamonds from his mother's dismantled tiara to design a diamond bracelet for his new wife. The Queen has worn the bracelet frequently throughout her reign. In recent years it has been borrowed by the Duchess of Cambridge. To mark their 5th wedding anniversary in 1952, Philip designed a gold bracelet which he commissioned Boucheron to create. The bracelet features Philip's Naval badge in diamonds surrounded by two sapphire crosses, perhaps representing the Greek flag. A ruby cross, perhaps representing the flag of England, is flanked by two roses of York symbolising the Queen's first title as Princess Elizabeth of York. All of these symbols are connected by gold links in the shape of interlocking Es and Ps. In 1966 Prince Philip purchased the "Venus" brooch as a gift for the Queen. The brooch is made of gold, carved rubies and diamonds, and was worn by the Queen for formal portraits commemorating her and Philip's 70th wedding anniversary in 2017. She has also worn this item since Philip's death as a tribute to her husband.

was a layperson when she met and then married Prince William, just as Queen Elizabeth the Queen Mother was when she met and married George VI, the tiara was likely a deliberate choice meant to pay homage to the Queen Mother herself. For her 2018 wedding to Prince Harry, Megan Markle loaned the Queen Mary Bandeau tiara, a royal family heirloom, from her grandmother-in-law to be.

Within the Queen's large collection of jewels, there are several items which have great sentimental significance. She is rarely seen in public without her favourite three-strand pearl necklace which was a gift from her beloved father, King George VI. It is said the Queen owns multiple pearl necklaces that are similar in

God Save Our Gracious Queen

In celebration of Her Majesty's 70 glorious years on the throne, a selection of memories and opinions from some of those who have had the honour of her presence and the privilege of meeting her. . .

'I have watched you grow up all these years with pride and I can, I know, always count on you to help us in our work'

Her 'loving papa' King George VI

Right:

Queen Elizabeth II and Prince Philip at Trooping the Colour, 2015

'I think I speak for my generation when I say that the example and continuity provided by The Queen is not only very rare among leaders but a great source of pride and reassurance'

The Duke of Cambridge

'I have seen Princess Elizabeth on several occasions since she became Queen. Her loveliness does not change but she seems to me still more serious, as one might expect her to be under the burden of her duties'

Eleanor Roosevelt, wife of American President Franklin D Roosevelt

'Lilibet is the only thing in this world which is absolutely real to me and my ambition is to wield the two of us into a new combined existence'

Prince Philip about his future wife shortly before their 1947 marriage

'The Queen looked absolutely ravishing. She had the most wonderful complexion and her eyes were glistening, and finally we, and the nation, set eyes on her exquisite Coronation dress. I have often been asked whether the Queen seemed nervous. She didn't – she was as calm as she always is. She had seen her father being crowned, and although she had been quite young, I am sure she would have remembered everything'

Lady Anne Coke, later Anne Glenconner, one of Elizabeth's Maids of Honour at the Coronation

---

'I was very impressed by the Queen. She had such a gentle, calm voice. She was completely unpretentious, completely without the hautiness that you'd expect of royalty. She may be the Queen of England but in our eyes she was first and foremost the wife of her husband and the mother of her children'

First Secretary of the Communist Party of the Soviet Union (1958-64), Nikita Khrushchev

---

'She is England personified'

French tourist Marie Le Verte

'Her Majesty brings to bear a formidable grasp of current issue and breadth of experience. And although the press could not resist the temptation to suggest disputes between the Palace and Downing Street, I always found the Queen's attitude towards the work of the Government absolutely correct'

Margaret Thatcher

'The Queen came over to lunch on Sunday, looking like a young girl. It was all very merry and agreeable but there is always, for me, a tiny pall of best behaviour overlaying the proceedings. I am not complaining about this, I think it is right and proper, but I am constantly aware of it. It isn't that I have a basic urge to tell disgusting jokes and say "f**k" every five minutes but I am conscious of a faint resentment that I couldn't if I wanted to. I told the Queen how moved I had been by Prince Charles' investiture, and she gaily shattered my sentimental illusions by saying that they were both struggling not to giggle because at the dress rehearsal the crown was too big and extinguished him like a candle snuffer!'

Noel Coward

'The Queen was quite shy, strangely so for someone of her experience and position, and at the same time, direct. I don't mean rude or insensitive but just direct. "You are my 10th prime minister," she said. "My first was Winston. That was before you were born'

Tony Blair

'A very pleasant middle to upper-class type of lady, with a talkative retired Navy husband'

Journalist and satirist Malcolm Muggeridge

'If she doesn't want to commit herself, she calls the dog'

Prince Philip

'The Queen has paved the way for the Royal Family to survive into the 21st century'

Harold Brooks Baker, royal historian, on Her Majesty's decision to pay tax

---

'The Empire has been replaced by the Commonwealth and the rate of social, industrial and technological change has been breath-taking. But through all this change, there has been the Queen – constant, reassuring, providing a sense of security and stability in an uncertain world, yet, remarkably, remaining in touch'

Former UK Foreign Secretary, Jack Straw

'When I got there the corgis walked in and in came Her Majesty and sat opposite me. It's one of those pinch-yourself moments you'll never forget for the rest of your life. We chatted about dogs and life, and the Queen was very polite but I don't remember exactly what I said because I was so nervous – you can't believe you're having a one-on-one conversation with the Queen for 45 minutes'

Celebrity chef James Martin on lunching with the Queen

'I was once at a shooting lunch. At the end of lunch, I heard someone say, "I'll do the washing-up." I turned round and there was the Queen in her yellow washing-up gloves'

An unnamed courtier of the Queen

'She is a symbol. But it's a very potent symbol. It's a symbol that carries the history of Britain

with it. And along with that a certain — a sense of continuity, obviously. And in her particular case, I think an incredible sense of self-discipline, which I suspect they all had, actually. I kind of love the Queen. I am Queenist'

Actress Dame Helen Mirren who won an Oscar for her portrayal of Elizabeth II in the 2006 film, 'The Queen'

'She is the rock 'n' roll queen. Weirdly enough, that is one of the things her reign will be remembered for. Queen Elizabeth I, we remember Raleigh; Queen Elizabeth II it's gonna be the Beatles'

Sir Paul McCartney

'I have a huge respect for the Queen and a lot of sympathy and compassion. I think she does amazing things for the United Kingdom. I really do'

Actress Claire Foy who played the Queen in the first two seasons of Netflix's 'The Crown'

'Her Majesty impressed me as someone who but for the circumstance of her birth, might have become a successful politician or diplomat. As it was, she had to be both, without quite seeming to be either'

President Bill Clinton wrote of the queen

'I spent an evening with the Queen, sitting on a sofa in the large living room, talking about our children like old friends'

Ronald Reagan

'As glamorous in her brogues and headscarf in Balmoral as she is wearing the crown jewels'

Vogue magazine

'The Top Lady'

Diana, Princess of Wales

'Having played the Queen, I have become slightly in love with her now. I think as far as royals go, she has such humility and a sort of stoicism that are very impressive'

Actress Olivia Colman who played Her Majesty in seasons 2-4 of Netflix's 'The Crown'

'It was inevitable, when there are two sisters and one is the Queen, who must be the source of honour and all that is good, while the other must be the focus of the most creative malice, the evil sister'

Her Majesty's sister, Princess Margaret

Right:
Sir Winston Churchill with Queen Elizabeth II, Prince Charles and Princess Anne, 10 February 1953

'She has a lovely laugh – she laughs with her whole face'

1960s Labour Minister, Richard Crossland

'The Queen has excellent legs!'

Former Labour MP, Dennis McShane

'The Queen certainly knows what's going on in the world of conservation and I think that she's genuinely concerned about it'

Sir David Attenborough

'Never have the august duties which fall upon the British monarch been discharged with more devotion than in the brilliant opening to your Majesty's reign. We thank God for the gift he has bestowed upon us and vow ourselves anew to the sacred cause, and wise and kindly way of life of which your Majesty is the young, gleaming champion' Sir Winston Churchill

'I was given this official list of 777 names – dignitaries, governors, all sorts of people – and not one person I knew. They said "These are the people we should invite". I looked at it in absolute horror and said "I think we should start again". I rang the Queen the next day and said "Do we need to be doing this?" And she said, "No, start with your friends first and go from there". And she told me to bin the list. She made the point that there are certain times when you have to strike the right balance. And it's advice like that which is really key, when you know that she's seen and done it all before'

Prince William on taking his granny's advice about who to invite to his 2011 wedding to Kate Middleton

---

'If you think of it, for so many years she has represented her country, she has really never made a mistake. You don't see, like, anything embarrassing. She is just an incredible woman'

Donald Trump

'I asked Her Majesty if she was going to the FA Cup final, she replied that she wasn't so I said, "Can I have your ticket, then?" Quick as a flash, she came back with "That's a Tommy Cooper joke,'

Madness singer Suggs on meeting the Queen at the Diamond Jubilee celebrations in 2012

'The Queen is a good, kind, devout lady. She looks after members of staff who look after her'

Former Royal butler, Paul Burrell

'The Queen must never appear to be chic. That would be disastrous, for there is an unkindness to chic, and Her Majesty must never appear to be unkind. She must always appear friendly and approachable'

Royal fashion designer Hardy Amies

'She is so much in a lot of our lives we know how she looks and sounds, of course, I have to be like her as much as I can but also tell a story and the story of her day'

Actress Imelda Staunton who is playing Her Majesty in the final two seasons of Netflix's 'The Crown'

'I have always liked the Queen. She's a human being. I have no problems with her at all. Long may she live'

John Lydon, formerly punk rocker Johnny Rotten, on Her Majesty. Quite a change of heart... Forty years earlier, he'd called her a 'Cardboard Cut-out'

Right:

This charming photograph was taken on the fourteenth birthday of Princess Elizabeth with her nine year old sister, Princess Margaret Rose, April 17th 1940

'The Queen is the only person who
can put on a tiara with one hand,
while walking down stairs'

Princess Margaret